Bon Appetit

Plancha

150 GREAT RECIPES FOR SPANISH-STYLE GRILLING

© Éditions Sud Ouest 2004

English translation copyright © 2011 Agate Publishing, Inc.

Printed in China

Originally published in France by Éditions Sud Ouest, 2004

All photographs by Pierre Bordet
Design by Brandtner Design.

Library of Congress Cataloging-in-Publication Data

Otal, Liliane.
[Plancha. English]
Plancha : 150 great recipes for Spanish-style grilling / Liliane Otal ; translated by Danielle McCumber.
     p. cm.
   Includes index.
   Summary: "A guide to the traditional style of Spanish flat-slab grilling, with recipes and photographs"--Provided by the publisher"-- Provided by publisher.
   ISBN-10: 1-57284-118-4 (flexibound)
   ISBN-13: 978-1-57284-118-5 (pbk.)
   1. Skillet cooking. 2. Cooking, Spanish. 3. Cookbooks. I. Title.
   TX840.S55O8313 2011
   641.5946–dc22

                    2011000422

11 12 13 14   10 9 8 7 6 5 4 3 2 1

Surrey Books is an imprint of Agate Publishing. Agate books are available in bulk at discount prices. For more information, go to agatepublishing.com.

Plancha

150 GREAT RECIPES FOR SPANISH-STYLE GRILLING

Liliane Otal

Photography by Pierre Bordet

SURREY BOOKS
AN AGATE IMPRINT
CHICAGO

CONTENTS

FIRST COURSES AND VEGETABLES............**48**

MEAT 124

POULTRY 148

INTRODUCTION

PLANCHA PASSION

Plancha is a Spanish word that literally means "plate." It usually refers to both the device and the mode of cooking: a flat metal sheet heated by a gas burner. This method of cooking is traditionally Spanish and forms part of that country's daily habits and culinary practices. Spaniards like to frequent bars and love to go out for a *paseo*, or short stroll, in the city along busy streets and squares, with relatives and friends of all ages.

The natural rhythm of these walks includes stops at tapas bars. Most bars have a plancha and offer small portions of prawns in garlic, mussels, fresh anchovies, *pulpitos* (cuttlefish) *chistorra* (a type of chorizo), or *pan con tomate* (bread rubbed with garlic and tomato sauce, heated on the plancha and served with a slice of ham). The plancha, usually visible from the bar, allows for the quick and efficient cooking of a great variety of foods.

Social gatherings increase greatly during *fiestas*: more than 25,000 "fetes" are celebrated in Spain every year, during which large planchas are set up in towns and village squares.

Spanish restaurants are especially fond of plancha cooking for refined dishes such as lobster tails, hake (similar to cod) steaks, *parilladas* of fish and shellfish, and rib-eye steaks.

However, the plancha is not reserved for professional cooks, and it has been a cultural favorite for a long time. Contrary to societies where people like to entertain small groups of friends at home, Spaniards tend to gather as members of culinary associations and gastronomical societies. These societies first formed in the nineteenth century, in the Basque province of Gipuzkoa in San Sebastian, then spread to neighboring provinces and on to all of Spain. They used to be exclusively male, but are now beginning to open up to women. The meeting place usually has a kitchen that features a prominent plancha. These societies now organize all sorts of activities—sporting events, conferences, and trips—but their main focus remains gastronomy.

THE RISE OF THE PLANCHA

For some years now, the plancha has been very popular in Spain, France and beyond. Professional cooks are unanimous in praising its merits and practicality—since food requires very little handling and no pots or pans it is simply laid on a heated plancha. In addition, food's natural flavors and nutritional value are preserved.

Some of the best chefs use planchas. For instance, famed French chef Paul Bocuse offers a "beef filet à la plancha" and a "fresh cod à la plancha" on his Brasserie menu. In his Paris restaurant Spoon, Alain Ducasse offers cuisine marked by American, Asian, and Latin influences, and he favors the plancha because it allows for fast cooking and to-the-minute preparations. At tapas and Spanish restaurants all over the United States a number of dishes are served "à la plancha."

From a technical point of view, the plancha is analogous to the griddle and to the Japanese *teppan yaki*. The griddle is a cooktop that can be flat or ridged; lighter than the plancha, it is popular in American fast-food restaurants. Its cooking temperature is lower than the plancha's and is perfect for cooking hamburgers. The plancha is heavier, thicker, and allows for more intense, quick heating.

Teppan yaki is a Japanese style of cooking used by professional chefs. The large heating surface is set right in front of customers, and chefs provide an entertaining show with their knives and ingredients.

A PLANCHA AT HOME

A plancha as it is sold in Europe is a cooktop made of metal: steel, stainless steel, or cast iron. It is rustproof since the plancha is meant to stay outdoors for a good part of the year.

The European plancha is not sold in the United States yet. However, manufacturers now sell planchas to be used on the grill or stovetop, including the Williams-Sonoma La Plancha Cast-Iron Griddle (sold at Williams -Sonoma); the Charcoal Companion Steven Raichlen Cast Iron Plancha (sold at Sears, Amazon.com, and the Steven Raichlen Barbecue Store); and the Fuego Element Griddle/Plancha Plate (sold at J.C. Penney, Walmart, and Buy. com). In the U.K., the plancha can be found at a few locations. The Garden Shop sells the Marco Pierre White Plancha, Made in Design offers a plancha for the Odeon 32 Grill, and Auravita sells the Carbone Plus Plancha Grill.

The recipes in this book were originally written for a large plancha surface, but can be used on other versions of the plancha easily; some recipes may need to be cooked in batches.

EVERYTHING GOES WITH PLANCHA

Practically anything can be cooked on the plancha. This book starts with marinade and sauce recipes, which can be used in a variety of plancha recipes (and are incorporated into several of the later chapters). Following chapters provide recipes for poultry, pork, beef, fish, seafood, vegetables, and desserts. Because the plancha brings out the natural flavors of food, the recipes in this book are for the most part simple, and don't need "dressing up." The dishes can be seasoned before, during, or after cooking, using marinades, sauces, spices, and condiments. Also, meat or fish can be cooked along with accompanying side dishes, which makes prep and cooking time short and simple, and allows the chef to visit with guests while preparing a delicious meal.

PLANCHA COOKING TIPS

- Oil the surface of the plancha before heating. Do not use butter, which burns at high temperature; butter can be added after cooking or served on the side, especially when flavored with parsley or anchovies (see recipes). To oil the surface, use a brush, a wad of cloth, or a paper towel.

- The plancha must be very hot or the food will stick to the surface.
  Set the temperature to its maximum level and keep it there for the
  duration of the cooking process because foods that are quickly seared
  are much tastier. Of course, overheating can cause food to burn and
  blacken. You must therefore learn to adjust the intensity of your plancha's heat to obtain the best results.

- Make sure ingredients are at room temperature: it is best to take them
  out of the refrigerator at least one hour before use. They will cook more
  evenly.

- Do not use wet ingredients. Be sure to pat dry the fish and vegetables
  that have just been washed.

- Only salt meat at the end of the cooking process to prevent juices from
  escaping. But do salt vegetables before cooking them: They will be
  more tender and cook more easily.

- Allow meat to rest for a few minutes, covered in aluminum foil before
  cutting into it after cooking. Only once it is removed from heat can
  juices begin to settle and the temperature spread more evenly from the
  outside in.

- Avoid using a knife directly on the plancha. Food must be carved
  first and readied for the plancha. To check the doneness of a piece of

meat, remove it from the plancha and put it on a plate before cutting into it. You will thus avoid burning yourself and damaging the plancha cooktop.

- Since plancha cooking is often fast, have all ingredients and utensils handy, and prepare the side dishes ahead of time. Guests must be ready to eat.

SAUCES AND MARINADES

GARLIC AND OLIVE OIL MARINADE

SERVES 6

- 1 CUP (236 ML) OLIVE OIL
- 4 CLOVES GARLIC, PEELED AND THINLY SLICED
- KOSHER SALT, TO TASTE
- PEPPER, TO TASTE

Pour olive oil into a small bowl and add garlic. Sprinkle generously with salt and pepper.

SERVING SUGGESTION: *This marinade can be used to coat any cut of beef, lamb, pork, or prawns. Let meat or seafood marinate for 3 hours before cooking.*

SPICY MARINADE

SERVES 6

- 5 TABLESPOONS (75 ML) OLIVE OIL
- 5 TABLESPOONS (75 ML) VINEGAR
- ½ TEASPOON (2.5 ML) CAYENNE PEPPER
- 2 CLOVES GARLIC, PEELED AND FINELY CHOPPED
- FRESH PARSLEY, FINELY CHOPPED, TO TASTE
- SALT, TO TASTE

Mix ingredients in a small bowl.

SERVING SUGGESTION: *This marinade can be used for any meat or fish. Let meat or fish marinate for 1 hour before cooking.*

CHINESE MARINADE

SERVES 6

- 6 TABLESPOONS (90 ML) SOY SAUCE
- 3 TABLESPOONS (45 ML) WALNUT OIL
- 3 TABLESPOONS (45 ML) VINEGAR
- 1 TEASPOON GRATED (5 ML) FRESH GINGER
- 1 SMALL BUNCH FRESH PARSLEY, FINELY CHOPPED
- PEPPER, TO TASTE

Mix ingredients in a small bowl.

SERVING SUGGESTION: *This marinade goes very well with fish and shellfish; it can also be used with pork. Let fish or meat marinate for 1 hour before cooking.*

21

EXOTIC MARINADE

SERVES 6

- 1½ CUPS (354 ML) PINEAPPLE JUICE
- 2 TABLESPOONS (30 ML) OIL
- 2 TABLESPOONS (30 ML) VINEGAR
- 2 CLOVES GARLIC, PEELED AND CHOPPED
- SALT, TO TASTE
- PEPPER, TO TASTE

Mix ingredients in a medium bowl.

SERVING SUGGESTION: *This works best for meat. Marinate for 2 hours before cooking.*

LIME MARINADE

- JUICE AND PEELS OF 6 LIMES
- SALT, TO TASTE
- WHITE PEPPER, TO TASTE

In a small bowl, combine all ingredients.

SERVING SUGGESTION: *Marinate fish 30 minutes to 1 hour before cooking, depending on the thickness. Marinating for too long will toughen fish.*

RUM MARINADE

SERVES 6

- 1 CUP (25 CL) RUM OR OTHER SWEET LIQUOR
- SALT, TO TASTE
- PEPPER, TO TASTE

Mix ingredients in small bowl.

SERVING SUGGESTION: *Use this with pork or chicken. Marinate meat for 2 hours before cooking.*

« WINE MARINADE

SERVES 6

- 1 CUP (25 CL) RED OR WHITE WINE
- 1 ONION, THINLY SLICED
- 1 CARROT, SLICED
- 2 CLOVES GARLIC, PEELED AND CRUSHED
- 2 BAY LEAVES
- 2 OR 3 SPRIGS FRESH THYME LEAVES
- SALT, TO TASTE
- PEPPER, TO TASTE

Mix ingredients in a medium bowl.

SERVING SUGGESTION: *This marinade, usually used for slow-cooked dishes, gives a wonderful flavor to meat cooked on the plancha. Marinating time is 4 hours.*

AIOLI

SERVES 6

- 6 CLOVES GARLIC, PEELED AND CRUSHED
- 1 EGG YOLK
- 1 CUP (20 CL) OLIVE OIL
- SALT, TO TASTE
- PEPPER, TO TASTE

Mix garlic with egg yolk then slowly begin to mix in the oil. When all of the oil has been mixed in, add salt and pepper.

SERVING SUGGESTION: *This sauce goes well with fish, shellfish, and vegetables.*

ASIAN MARINADE »

SERVES 6

- 1 BUNCH FRESH CILANTRO, CHOPPED
- 4 CLOVES GARLIC, PEELED AND CHOPPED
- JUICE OF 2 LEMONS
- 1 TEASPOON (5 ML) CUMIN
- 2 TEASPOONS (10 ML) SWEET CHILI PEPPER, MINCED
- ½ TEASPOON (1 ¼ ML) SPICY CHILI PEPPER, MINCED
- 4 TABLESPOONS (60 ML) OIL
- 4 TABLESPOONS (60 ML) WATER
- SALT, TO TASTE

Mix ingredients in medium bowl.

SERVING SUGGESTION: *Use this marinade with fish. Let fish marinate for 2 hours before cooking.*

BASIL MARINADE

SERVES 6

- 1 CUP (25 CL) OLIVE OIL
- 1 BUNCH FRESH BASIL LEAVES
- SALT, TO TASTE
- PEPPER, TO TASTE

Soak basil leaves in olive oil for at least 24 hours. Add salt and pepper.

SERVING SUGGESTION: *This marinade goes well with meat, poultry, fish, or vegetables. Marinating time is 2 hours.*

COCONUT MARINADE

SERVES 6

- 1 (8.5-OUNCE [25-CL]) CAN COCONUT MILK
- 2 CLOVES GARLIC, PEELED AND CHOPPED
- 1 TOMATO, DICED
- 1 PINCH CAYENNE PEPPER
- SALT, TO TASTE

Pour coconut milk into a medium bowl and mix in the garlic, tomato, cayenne pepper, and salt.

SERVING SUGGESTION: *This marinade goes well with seafood or chicken. Let meat or fish marinate for 2 hours before cooking.*

HONEY MARINADE

SERVES 6

- 2 TABLESPOONS (30 ML) OIL
- 2 TABLESPOONS (30 ML) VINEGAR
- 1 TEASPOON (5 ML) TOMATO PURÉE
- 2 TABLESPOONS (30 ML) WORCESTERSHIRE SAUCE
- 2 TABLESPOONS (30 ML) HONEY
- 1 TABLESPOON (15 ML) SOY SAUCE
- 1 PINCH CHILI POWDER
- 2 CLOVES GARLIC, PEELED AND CHOPPED
- SALT, TO TASTE
- PEPPER, TO TASTE

Mix ingredients in small bowl.

SERVING SUGGESTION: *This marinade is great with pork, duck breasts, and chicken wings. Let meat marinate for 2 hours before cooking.*

MAYONNAISE WITH HERBS

SERVES 6

- 1 EGG YOLK
- 1 TABLESPOON (15 ML) MUSTARD
- 1½ TABLESPOON (22 ML) SUNFLOWER OIL
- SALT, TO TASTE
- PEPPER, TO TASTE
- 3 FRESH BASIL LEAVES, JULIENNED
- 3 SPRIGS FRESH PARSLEY, CHOPPED
- 3 SPRIGS FRESH THYME LEAVES
- 1 TEASPOON (5 ML) VINEGAR

In a bowl, whip the egg yolk then add mustard and mix well. Add some drops of oil and continue to whip. As the mayonnaise thickens, slowly pour in the rest of the oil while whipping. Add salt, pepper, herbs, and vinegar. Mix well.

SERVING SUGGESTION: *This sauce goes well with fish, shellfish, poultry, and other white meats.*

VARIATION: *The vinegar can be replaced with the same quantity of lemon juice.*

BBQ SAUCE

SERVES 6

- **2** TABLESPOONS (**30** ML) VINEGAR
- **2** TABLESPOONS (**30** ML) OIL
- **3** TABLESPOONS (**45** ML) KETCHUP
- **1** TABLESPOON (**15** ML) MUSTARD
- **1** TABLESPOON (**15** ML) SUGAR
- **2** CLOVES GARLIC, PEELED AND FINELY CHOPPED
- SALT, TO TASTE
- PEPPER, TO TASTE

Mix ingredients well and serve cold with any type of meat.

CREAMY GARLIC SAUCE

SERVES 6
COOKING TIME: 10 MINUTES

- 4 CLOVES GARLIC, PEELED
- JUICE OF 1 LEMON
- 2 TABLESPOONS (30 ML) MAYONNAISE
- SALT, TO TASTE
- 1 TEASPOON (5 ML) PAPRIKA
- ½ CUP (118 ML) CREAM

1. Place garlic in a small pot and cover with water. Bring to a boil and cook over a small flame for about 10 minutes. Drain garlic and carefully crush with a mortar and pestle.

2. In a medium bowl, mix lemon juice, mayonnaise, salt, and paprika. Set aside.

3. Whisk cream in an electric mixer to the consistency of whipped cream. Slowly add it to the lemon and garlic sauce.

SERVING SUGGESTION: *This sauce goes well with meat, especially red meat.*

ANCHOVY BUTTER

SERVES 6

- ¾ CUP (150 G) SALTED ANCHOVIES
- ¾ CUP (150 G) BUTTER
- PEPPER, TO TASTE

1. Desalinate the anchovies by soaking them in water for about 10 minutes. Rinse well. Remove the tails and backbones. Towel dry and cut into pieces.

2. Crush anchovies and butter with a mortar and pestle to create a paste. Add pepper to taste. Place in refrigerator in a small container.

SERVING SUGGESTION: *This butter is a perfect accompaniment to fish and vegetables.*

« PARSLEY BUTTER

SERVES 6

- 2 CLOVES GARLIC, PEELED AND CRUSHED
- 1 SMALL BUNCH FRESH PARSLEY, CHOPPED
- ¾ CUP (150 G) BUTTER
- SALT, TO TASTE
- PEPPER, TO TASTE

1. Crush garlic and parsley together with a mortar and pestle.

2. Mix with butter, salt, and pepper until a paste is achieved.

3. Place in refrigerator in a small container.

SERVING SUGGESTION: *Parsley butter goes very well with red meat.*

PINK ONION BUTTER

SERVES 6

- 1 PINK ONION, CHOPPED
- ¾ CUP (150 G) BUTTER
- SALT, TO TASTE
- PEPPER, TO TASTE

1. Crush onion with a mortar and pestle. In a small bowl, mix with butter, salt, and pepper.

2. Continue to mash with pestle until mixture is the consistency of paste, then transfer to a small container and place in refrigerator.

SERVING SUGGESTION: *This butter is best with poultry, fish, and vegetables.*

CURRY SAUCE »

SERVES 6
COOKING TIME: 10 MINUTES

- 2 ONIONS, MINCED
- OLIVE OIL
- 2 TEASPOONS (10 ML) CURRY POWDER
- ½ CUP (118 ML) WHITE WINE
- 2 TABLESPOONS (30 ML) CREAM
- SALT, TO TASTE
- PEPPER, TO TASTE

1. Brown the onions with a little olive oil in a large pot for 5 minutes over low heat.

2. Add curry powder and wine and let simmer for 2 minutes.

3. Add cream. Stir well, adding salt and pepper, and heat for another 2 to 3 minutes.

SERVING SUGGESTION: *Serve curry sauce hot with fish or poultry.*

LEMON BUTTER SAUCE

SERVES 6
COOKING TIME: 5 MINUTES

- JUICE OF 3 LEMONS
- 1 TABLESPOON (15 ML) FRESH CHIVES, CHOPPED
- ½ CUP (100 G) BUTTER, CUT INTO MEDIUM-SIZED PIECES

1. Pour lemon juice into a small pot. Add chives and cook over low heat for 3 minutes.

2. Add butter and let melt for 2 to 3 minutes while stirring over low heat.

SERVING SUGGESTION: *This butter sauce is best served hot with fish.*

VARIATION: *To thicken into a heartier sauce, add flour or egg yolk.*

SPICY TOMATO SAUCE

SERVES 6
COOKING TIME: 38 MINUTES

- 1 ONION, ROUGHLY CHOPPED
- 1 CLOVE GARLIC, PEELED AND ROUGHLY CHOPPED
- OLIVE OIL
- 5 RIPE TOMATOES, PEELED, SEEDED, AND CUT INTO CUBES
- SALT, TO TASTE
- PEPPER, TO TASTE
- 1 TEASPOON (5 ML) SUGAR
- 1 SMALL BUNCH FRESH BASIL, CHOPPED
- 1 PINCH HOT CHILI POWDER

1. Brown onion and garlic in a large skillet with a bit of olive oil over low heat. Add tomatoes, salt, pepper, sugar, basil, and chili powder.

2. Stir sauce well and simmer for 30 minutes until it is very thick.

SERVING SUGGESTION: *This sauce can be served hot or cold, and it goes with meat, poultry, and vegetables.*

ROQUEFORT SAUCE

SERVES 6

- ½ CUP (100 G) ROQUEFORT CHEESE
- JUICE OF 1 LEMON
- PEPPER, TO TASTE
- 3 TABLESPOONS (45 ML) CREAM

Using a fork, mix Roquefort and lemon juice until a consistent paste is formed. Add pepper and cream.

SERVING SUGGESTION: *This sauce can be served cold with vegetables or hot with meat (it's particularly good with red meat).*

36

PINK SAUCE

SERVES 6

- 1 EGG YOLK
- 1 TEASPOON (5 ML) MUSTARD
- 1 CUP (20 CL) SUNFLOWER OIL
- 1 TABLESPOON (15 ML) VINEGAR
- 1 TABLESPOON (15 ML) KETCHUP
- SALT, TO TASTE
- PEPPER, TO TASTE

1. In a bowl, whisk egg yolk and mustard until they are mixed well. Add a few drops of oil and continue to whisk.

2. As the sauce thickens, slowly pour in the rest of the oil, continuing all the while to whisk. Add the vinegar, ketchup, salt, and pepper. Mix well.

SERVING SUGGESTION: *This sauce works well with shellfish.*

PESTO

SERVES 6

- 4 CLOVES GARLIC, PEELED AND CHOPPED
- 1 BUNCH FRESH BASIL LEAVES, CHOPPED
- ½ POUND (200 G) SWISS CHEESE, GRATED
- ½ CUP (118 ML) OLIVE OIL
- SALT, TO TASTE
- PEPPER, TO TASTE

1. Mash garlic, basil, and cheese with a mortar and pestle.

2. Add oil until a thick sauce is achieved. Add salt and pepper.

SERVING SUGGESTION: *This pesto goes well with vegetables, pork, and poultry.*

GUACAMOLE

SERVES 6

- 2 RIPE AVOCADOS
- 1 TOMATO, FINELY CHOPPED
- 1 ONION, FINELY CHOPPED
- ½ CLOVE GARLIC, PEELED AND FINELY CHOPPED
- 1 HANDFUL FRESH CILANTRO LEAVES, FINELY CHOPPED
- 2 TABLESPOONS (30 ML) CREAM
- JUICE OF 1 LEMON
- SALT, TO TASTE
- HOT SAUCE, TO TASTE

1. Cut avocados in half and remove pits. Peel avocadoes and mash with a fork in a medium bowl.

2. Separately, mix tomato, onion, garlic, and cilantro. Add mixture to the avocado and mix well.

3. Add cream, lemon juice, a little salt and hot sauce. Blend well to create a smooth texture.

SERVING SUGGESTION: *Guacamole goes well with vegetables, poultry, or white meat.*

MANGO CHUTNEY

SERVES 6
COOKING TIME: 15 MINUTES

- 2 MANGOES, PEELED, PITTED, AND DICED
- ½ CUP (100 G) RAISINS
- 1 CLOVE GARLIC, PEELED AND CHOPPED
- 2 TABLESPOONS (30 ML) SUGAR
- 2 TABLESPOONS (30 ML) VINEGAR
- JUICE OF 1 LEMON
- SALT, TO TASTE
- PEPPER, TO TASTE

1. Put mangoes, raisins, garlic, sugar, and vinegar in a medium pot and season with lemon juice, salt, and pepper. Cook over low heat for 15 minutes, stirring frequently.

2. When the liquid has evaporated, pour chutney into a jar and let cool.

SERVING SUGGESTION: *Serve chilled with meat or poultry.*

TOMATO "ROUGAIL"

SERVES 6

This Creole sauce has many variations, but always starts with a base of tomatoes, ginger, and chili pepper. It originated in the French territories of the Indian Ocean.

- 6 TOMATOES, PEELED, SEEDED, AND CRUSHED
- 2 ONIONS, CHOPPED
- 1 RED CHILI PEPPER, GROUND OR ½ TEASPOON (2.5 ML) RED PEPPER FLAKES
- 1 TEASPOON (5 ML) GROUND GINGER
- SALT, TO TASTE

Mix all ingredients into a sauce.

SERVING SUGGESTION: *Serve as a condiment to meat.*

ONION COMPOTE

SERVES 6
COOKING TIME: 21 MINUTES

- BUTTER TO SAUTÉ ONIONS
- 4 PURPLE ONIONS, MINCED
- 1 TABLESPOON (15 ML) VINEGAR
- 2 TABLESPOONS (30 ML) WATER
- SALT, TO TASTE
- PEPPER, TO TASTE
- 1 TABLESPOON (15 ML) SUGAR

1. Melt a small amount of butter in a pot. Add onions and cook until transparent, about 10 minutes. Add vinegar, water, salt, and pepper. Cover and let cook 10 more minutes.

2. When liquid has completely evaporated, sprinkle with sugar and cook 1 more minute while stirring, until sugar is caramelized.

SERVING SUGGESTION: *Onion compote can be served warm or cold.*

GREEN SAUCE

SERVES 6
COOKING TIME: 11 MINUTES

- 2 CLOVES GARLIC, PEELED AND FINELY CHOPPED
- 1 BUNCH FRESH PARSLEY, FINELY CHOPPED
- 1 TO 2 TABLESPOONS (15 TO 30 ML) OLIVE OIL
- 1 TEASPOON (5 ML) FLOUR
- 1 CUP (25 CL) WHITE WINE
- SALT, TO TASTE
- PEPPER, TO TASTE

Brown garlic and parsley in oil for 1 minute in a small pot over low heat. Sprinkle in flour and add wine, salt, and pepper. Simmer over low heat for about 10 minutes.

SERVING SUGGESTION: *Serve hot with fish.*

MUSHROOM SAUCE

SERVES 6
COOKING TIME: 15 MINUTES

- 1 TABLESPOON (15 ML) OLIVE OIL
- 1 (14-OUNCE [400 G]) CAN MUSHROOMS, DRAINED AND CHOPPED
- A FEW SPRIGS OF FRESH PARSLEY, CHOPPED
- SALT, TO TASTE
- 1 TABLESPOON (15 ML) FLOUR
- 1 LADLEFUL HOT CHICKEN STOCK
- 1 CUP (236 ML) WHITE WINE
- PEPPER, TO TASTE

1. Over medium heat, cook olive oil, mushrooms, parsley, and a dash of salt for 5 minutes.

2. Sprinkle mixture with flour then pour in chicken stock and wine. Mix well and simmer for about 10 minutes.

3. Add salt and pepper. When the sauce is of a medium-thick consistency, remove from heat.

SERVING SUGGESTION: *Serve hot with pork or chicken.*

"DOG" SAUCE

SERVES 6

Sauce chien, *or dog sauce, is a traditional French West Indies spicy sauce.
It is not known where it got its unusual name, though some attribute it to the
"bite" of the pepper.*

- 2 ONIONS, FINELY CHOPPED
- 2 CLOVES GARLIC, PEELED AND FINELY CHOPPED
- 1 SMALL BUNCH FRESH PARSLEY, CHOPPED
- SALT, TO TASTE
- 1 PINCH CAYENNE PEPPER
- 1 CUP (236 ML) BOILING WATER
- JUICE OF 1 LEMON

Mix onions, garlic, and parsley in a medium bowl. Add salt and cayenne
pepper. Add boiling water then lemon juice, and let mixture sit a couple of
minutes to infuse the flavors.

SERVING SUGGESTION: *Serve with fish cooked on the plancha.*

TAPENADE (PHOTO ON PP. 18-19)

SERVES 6

- **12 SALTED ANCHOVIES**
- **¾ POUND (300 G) BLACK OLIVES, SEEDS REMOVED**
- **½ POUND (200 G) CAPERS**
- **1 CLOVE GARLIC, PEELED AND CRUSHED**
- **1 SPRIG FRESH THYME LEAVES**
- **1 TEASPOON (5 ML) MUSTARD**
- **2 TABLESPOONS (30 ML) COGNAC**
- **OLIVE OIL, TO TASTE**
- **PEPPER, TO TASTE**

1. Desalinate the anchovies by soaking them in water for about 10 minutes. Rinse well. Remove the tails and backbones. Towel dry and cut into small pieces.

2. Mash anchovies, olives, capers, and garlic in a large bowl. Add thyme, mustard, and cognac.

3. Continue to mash mixture until a thick, smooth paste is achieved. Slowly add in oil and pepper as desired.

SERVING SUGGESTION: *Tapenade goes well with vegetables, fish, or meat.*

CREAM CHEESE PESTO

SERVES 6

- 4 CLOVES GARLIC, PEELED
- 1 BUNCH FRESH BASIL, CHOPPED
- ½ POUND (200 G) SWISS CHEESE, GRATED (OPTIONAL)
- 4 TABLESPOONS (60 ML) CREAM CHEESE
- SALT, TO TASTE
- PEPPER, TO TASTE

1. Mash garlic, basil, and Swiss cheese with a mortar and pestle.

2. Mix in cream cheese. Add salt and pepper and mix well.

NOTE: *This pesto sauce is lighter than the classic version.*

PEANUT SAUCE

SERVES 6

- ¼ POUND (100 G) PEANUTS, SHELLED, AND GROUND
- 1 ONION, CHOPPED
- 1 CLOVE GARLIC, PEELED AND CHOPPED
- 1 TEASPOON (5 ML) SUGAR
- 1 TABLESPOON (15 ML) VINEGAR
- 2 TABLESPOONS (30 ML) HEAVY CREAM
- HOT SAUCE, TO TASTE
- SALT, TO TASTE

1. Mix peanuts, onion, and garlic in medium bowl.

2. Add sugar, vinegar, cream, and a couple drops of hot sauce.

3. Add salt and mix well.

SERVING SUGGESTION: *This sauce should be served with beef.*

DILL SAUCE

SERVES 6

- 1 BUNCH FRESH DILL LEAVES, CHOPPED
  OR 1 TABLESPOON (15 ML) DRIED DILL LEAVES
- 2 EGGS, HARDCOOKED, SHELLED, AND CHOPPED
- 1 TEASPOON (5 ML) MUSTARD
- 2 TABLESPOONS (30 ML) OLIVE OIL
- JUICE OF 1 LEMON
- SALT, TO TASTE
- PEPPER, TO TASTE

1. Mix dill and eggs in a medium bowl.

2. Add mustard and olive oil. Mix well.

3. Add lemon juice, salt, and pepper, and mix.

SERVING SUGGESTION: *This sauce should be served with fish.*

FIRST COURSES AND VEGETABLES

HABAÑEROS

SERVES 6
COOKING TIME: 5 MINUTES

- **12** SLICES WHITE BREAD
- BUTTER TO COVER BREAD SLICES
- **6** SLICES HAM
- **6** SLICES CHEDDAR CHEESE
- OIL
- **6** EGGS
- SALT, TO TASTE
- PEPPER, TO TASTE

1. Using an upside-down glass, cut a circle roughly 2-inch hole (6 cm) in diameter out of 6 of the bread slices; discard the circles. Butter both sides of all remaining bread slices (including those with holes) and place the six whole slices on the plancha.

2. After a few seconds, turn the bread and place one slice of ham and one slice of cheese on each. Move these slices to one side of the plancha.

3. Oil the middle of the plancha lightly and fry the eggs for about 3 minutes. Add salt and pepper to taste. When the eggs are cooked, move the bread with ham and cheese on them to a plate, and carefully place an egg on each one.

4. Place the bread slices with holes on the plancha and toast for just a few seconds on each side, until golden brown. Then move these slices on top of the eggs so that the egg yolks appear in the holes. Serve immediately.

NOTE: *The habañeros may need to be cooked in batches depending on the size of the plancha and the number of servings needed.*

ANCHOVY TOAST

SERVES 6
COOKING TIME: 5 MINUTES

- 3 (2-OUNCE [43-G]) CANS ANCHOVIES IN OIL
- 6 SLICES FRENCH BREAD
- 3 TOMATOES, SLICED
- 6 THIN SLICES SWISS CHEESE
- 1 SPRIG FRESH THYME LEAVES

1. Pour anchovies with oil into a bowl and mash.

2. Place bread and tomatoes on the plancha. After a couple seconds, turn bread and spread with crushed anchovies. Cover with a slice of cheese.

3. Cook tomatoes 2 minutes on each side, then place 3 slices on each piece of bread.

4. Sprinkle with thyme and serve.

TOAST WITH CHICKEN AND HAM

(PHOTO ON PP. 48-49)

SERVES 6
COOKING TIME: 7 MINUTES

- **3** CHICKEN BREASTS, CUT INTO STRIPS
- **2** CLOVES GARLIC, PEELED AND PRESSED
- SALT, TO TASTE
- PAPRIKA, TO TASTE
- **6** SLICES SERRANO HAM
- OLIVE OIL
- **6** SLICES WHITE BREAD
- **6** PICKLED CHILI PEPPERS

1. In a medium or large bowl, mix chicken strips, garlic, salt, and paprika. Let sit for 30 minutes.

2. Cook chicken on the plancha, flipping frequently, for 5 minutes. When the chicken strips are cooked, move them to a corner of the plancha.

3. Cook ham slices on the plancha, just a couple seconds on each side, then put to the side with the chicken.

4. Drizzle oil on the bread slices and place on the plancha to toast, just a few seconds on each side. Set them on a plate.

5. Put a slice of ham on each piece of toast, then cover with chicken. Add the pickled chili peppers and serve.

CHORIZO TOAST

SERVES 6
COOKING TIME: 4 MINUTES

- 6 SLICES FRENCH BREAD
- 18 SMALL SWEET PEPPERS
- SALT, TO TASTE
- 1 LARGE SPANISH CHORIZO LINK (ABOUT 3 INCHES [8 CM] DIAMETER) AND CUT INTO $1/3$-INCH-THICK (0.8-CM-THICK) SLICES

1. Toast bread on the plancha for 2 minutes on each side, then move to a plate.

2. Cook the sweet peppers for 2 minutes on each side. Add salt.

3. One minute before the sweet peppers are finished cooking, cook the chorizo at most for 30 seconds on each side.

4. Place chorizo on the bread (about 3 pieces per slice), then cover with sweet peppers.

ITALIAN TOAST

SERVE 6
COOKING TIME: 7 MINUTES

- **6** GREEN BELL PEPPERS, SLICED
- **6** TOMATOES, SLICED
- SALT, TO TASTE
- PEPPER, TO TASTE
- **6** SLICES FRENCH BREAD
- **12** SLICES MOZZARELLA CHEESE
- OLIVE OIL, TO TASTE

1. Cook peppers and tomatoes on the plancha for 2 to 3 minutes on each side. Put the tomatoes on last because they cook faster than green bell peppers. Add salt and pepper.

2. Toast the bread for 1 minute on each side. Drizzle with olive oil.

3. Place a couple slices of tomato and green bell pepper on each piece of bread. Place 2 slices of mozzarella on top and heat 1 minute more.

SERVING SUGGESTION: *Have olive oil (preferably Italian) at the table to allow your guests to add it as they desire.*

TOAST WITH SAUSAGE AND MUSTARD

SERVES 6
COOKING TIME: 8 MINUTES

- 3 ONIONS, SLICED
- OLIVE OIL
- 6 STRASBOURG SAUSAGES, SLICED IN HALF LENGTHWISE
- 6 SLICES WHITE BREAD
- 12 CORNICHONS (BABY GHERKINS), CHOPPED
- 1 TABLESPOON (15 ML) MUSTARD
- SALT, TO TASTE

1. Cook onions for 2 to 3 minutes on each side, drizzling with oil as they cook. Once they are a golden color, move onions to a corner of the plancha.

2. Heat the sausage halves for 1 minute on each side. At the same time, toast the bread slices for 1 minute on each side.

3. Mix *cornichons* with the mustard. Spread one side of bread slices with the *cornichons*-mustard mixture.

4. Cover with onions and sausage halves. Serve immediately.

MEDITERRANEAN TOAST

SERVES 6
COOKING TIME: 6 MINUTES

- **6** SMALL TOMATOES, SLICED
- **6** SLICES FRENCH BREAD
- **6** SLICES GOAT CHEESE
- **6** FRESH BASIL LEAVES
- SALT, TO TASTE
- PEPPER, TO TASTE
- OLIVE OIL

1. Cook tomato slices for 2 minutes on each side.

2. Toast bread slices for 1 minute then remove from the plancha.

3. Put tomato slices on toasted side of the bread and then top off with one slice of goat cheese.

4. Put one basil leaf on each slice of toast. Heat on the plancha 2 minutes.

5. Add salt, pepper, and a drizzle of olive oil before serving.

TALOA

SERVES 6
COOKING TIME: 6 MINUTES

Taloa is a typical Basque recipe for flatbread made from wheat and corn flour. The dough must rest 1 hour; if time is an issue you can always substitute with whole-wheat pitas.

- ¾ POUND (300 G) WHOLE WHEAT FLOUR
- ¾ POUND (300 G) CORN FLOUR
- SALT, TO TASTE
- 1 CUP (25 CL) WATER
- BACON, HAM, RENDERED FAT (PORK, DUCK, CHICKEN), OR *FROMAGE DE BREBIS* (CREAMY SHEEP'S MILK CHEESE)

1. Mix the flours together in a large bowl. Add two pinches of salt. Pour in water and mix until a firm dough is achieved.

2. Roll dough into a ball and let sit for 1 hour.

3. Divide the dough into 6 equal parts, then flatten with a rolling pin into semi-thick circles.

4. Cook the *taloa* slices on the plancha for 2 to 3 minutes on each side.

5. At the same time, cook the bacon, ham, fat, or *fromage de brebis*. Serve with topping of your choice.

PAN CON TOMATE

SERVES 6
COOKING TIME: 2 MINUTES

- **6** THICK SLICES FRENCH BREAD
- **2** CLOVES GARLIC, PEELED AND HALVED
- **1** TOMATO, CUT IN HALF
- KOSHER SALT, TO TASTE
- OLIVE OIL
- **6** SLICES HAM

1. Toast bread on the plancha for 1 minute on each side. Rub slices with garlic, then with a tomato half.

2. Add a small amount of salt and olive oil to the bread.

3. Place ham on the still-hot bread. Serve immediately. The temperature of the bread will lightly heat the ham.

VARIATION: *The ham can also be cooked on the plancha at the same time as the bread.*

MANCHEGO À LA PLANCHA

SERVES 6
COOKING TIME: 1 MINUTE

Manchego is a hard cheese from the Spanish region of Mancha.

- ¾ POUND (300 G) FIELD GREENS
- OLIVE OIL, TO TASTE
- SHERRY VINEGAR, TO TASTE
- SALT, TO TASTE
- PEPPER, TO TASTE
- 6 MEDIUM-THICK SLICES MANCHEGO CHEESE

1. Season the field greens with olive oil, sherry vinegar, salt, and pepper. Mix well and place some salad on each plate.

2. Heat cheese slices on the plancha for 30 seconds on each side. Put cheese on top of the salads and serve.

MEXICAN TOSTADAS

SERVES 6
COOKING TIME: 10 MINUTES

- 1½ POUNDS (600 G) PEELED FROZEN SHRIMP, THAWED
- 2 CLOVES GARLIC, PEELED AND CHOPPED
- 1 SMALL BUNCH FRESH PARSLEY, CHOPPED
- ½ TABLESPOON (7 ML) CUMIN
- SALT, TO TASTE
- PEPPER, TO TASTE
- OLIVE OIL, TO TASTE
- 6 FLOUR OR CORN TORTILLAS
- 3 TABLESPOONS (45 ML) OIL
- 1 TOMATO, CHOPPED
- LETTUCE LEAVES, SHREDDED

1. Place shrimp in a bowl with garlic and parsley. Sprinkle with cumin, salt, pepper, and oil. Mix well and let sit 30 minutes before cooking.

2. Use half of the plancha to heat the tortillas, approximately 1 minute each side, and the other side to cook the drained shrimp for 5 minutes, flipping frequently.

3. Put tortillas on a serving dish or directly on your guests' plates. Place shrimp on top of the tortillas. Serve tomato and lettuce on the side.

SERVING SUGGESTION: *Can be served with Spicy Tomato Sauce (p. 36).*

TOSTADAS DEL MAR

SERVES 6
COOKING TIME: 10 MINUTES

- 2 POUNDS (1 KG) FRESH MUSSELS, WASHED
- 3 ONIONS, SLICED
- 6 SLICES FRENCH BREAD
- 2 (2-OUNCE [43-G]) CANS ANCHOVIES IN OIL
- ZEST AND JUICE OF 1 LEMON

1. Cook mussels in large pot of boiling water until shells open. Remove shells and set mussels aside.

2. Heat onion slices for 2 to 3 minutes on each side.

3. Toast bread slices for 1 minute on each side, then remove from the plancha.

4. Place onion slices, mussels, and anchovies on top of bread. Decorate with lemon zest and heat 2 minutes.

5. Sprinkle with lemon juice and serve.

CRUNCHY SAUSAGE

SERVES 6
COOKING TIME: 6 MINUTES

- 6 BLOOD SAUSAGES, CUT INTO THICK SLICES
- 1 LOAF FRENCH BREAD, CUT INTO SLICES
- MUSTARD TO COVER BREAD SLICES

1. Cook the sausage on the plancha for 3 minutes on each side.

2. Two minutes before the sausage is done cooking, toast the bread slices on each side on the plancha.

3. Remove bread and lightly cover slices with mustard.

4. Place one piece of sausage on top of each slice, using a toothpick to hold everything together.

SERVING SUGGESTION: *Serve as an appetizer.*

64

CHISTORRA

SERVES 6
COOKING TIME: 8 MINUTES

Chistorra *is a thin red sausage, similar to chorizo.*

- 1½ POUNDS (600 G) *CHISTORRA,* CUT INTO 1-INCH (2-CM) PIECES
- 1 LOAF FRENCH BREAD, CUT INTO SLICES

1. Cook *chistorra* pieces about 8 minutes on the plancha, turning often.

2. Two minutes before the sausage is done, toast the bread slices both sides on the plancha.

3. Remove bread and place a piece of *chistorra* on each slice, using a toothpick to hold everything together.

SERVING SUGGESTION: *Serve as an appetizer.*

SARDINE-STUFFED PEPPERS

SERVES 6
COOKING TIME: 16 MINUTES

- 6 GREEN OR RED BELL PEPPERS, CUT IN HALF LENGTHWISE, SEEDS AND STEMS REMOVED
- 24 SARDINE FILETS
- SALT, TO TASTE
- PEPPER, TO TASTE
- 3 SPRIGS FRESH THYME LEAVES
- 12 GREEN AND BLACK OLIVES, PITTED AND CHOPPED
- SWEET VINEGAR, TO TASTE

1. Cook peppers for 6 to 8 minutes on each side, turning occasionally.

2. About halfway through cooking peppers, cook sardines for 2 to 3 minutes on each side.

3. Add salt and pepper.

4. Place 2 sardine filets in each pepper half. Sprinkle with thyme and olives. Drizzle with sweet vinegar and serve.

ENDIVES À LA PLANCHA

SERVES 6
COOKING TIME: 10 MINUTES

- OLIVE OIL
- 12 ENDIVE LEAVES, HALVED LENGTHWISE
- SALT, TO TASTE
- PEPPER, TO TASTE
- PESTO (P. 37)

1. Lightly oil the endive leaves and cook on the plancha for about 10 minutes.

2. Add salt and pepper, and turn frequently. Serve with Pesto.

ESCARGOTS À LA PLANCHA

SERVES 6
COOKING TIME: 15 MINUTES

- 2 POUNDS (1 KG) CANNED OR FROZEN ESCARGOTS
- 2 CLOVES GARLIC, PEELED AND CHOPPED
- OLIVE OIL, TO TASTE
- SALT, TO TASTE
- PEPPER, TO TASTE
- VINEGAR, TO TASTE

1. Cook escargot on the plancha for about 10 minutes.

2. Two minutes before escargot are done cooking, sprinkle with garlic and olive oil.

3. Add salt and pepper, and sprinkle with vinegar. Serve hot.

BABY ARTICHOKES À LA PLANCHA

SERVES 6
COOKING TIME: 26 MINUTES

- **24** BABY ARTICHOKE HEARTS, WASHED AND CUT INTO THIN STRIPS LENGTHWISE
- SALT, TO TASTE
- PEPPER, TO TASTE
- $^1/_3$ POUND (**150** G) THIN SLICES OF HAM, PREFERABLY IBERICO
- OLIVE OIL, TO TASTE

1. Cook the artichoke heart strips 1 to 2 minutes on each side.

2. Add salt and pepper. Put them on a plate then cover with the slices of ham. Let ham warm up from the artichokes for 2 minutes.

3. Drizzle with oil and serve.

« GOLDEN PESTO VEGETABLES

SERVES 6
COOKING TIME: 10 MINUTES

- 3 ZUCCHINIS, WASHED, DRIED,
  AND CUT INTO STRIPS LENGTHWISE
- 3 EGGPLANTS, WASHED, DRIED,
  AND CUT INTO STRIPS LENGTHWISE
- 3 TOMATOES, CUT IN HALF
- 3 BELL PEPPERS, SLICED
- ⅔ CUP (120 ML) GREEK YOGURT
- PESTO (P. 37)

1. Heat vegetables on the plancha for about 10 to 15 minutes, turning occasionally. Remove tomatoes from heat first, as they cook fastest.

2. When all the vegetables have been cooked, place them on a serving dish. Add Greek yogurt to the Pesto, mix well and pour over the vegetables.

PARMESAN ZUCCHINI

SERVES 6
COOKING TIME: 4 MINUTES

- 3 ZUCCHINIS, UNPEELED, SLICED
- 1 (5-OUNCE [140-G]) TUB GRATED PARMESAN CHEESE
- PEPPER, TO TASTE
- OLIVE OIL, TO TASTE

1. Cook zucchini 2 minutes on the plancha then turn them over. Sprinkle with Parmesan and pepper and cook another 2 minutes.

2. Place zucchini on a platter and drizzle with olive oil.

NOTE: *No need to salt the zucchini, because the Parmesan is enough.*

VARIATION: *Fruit-infused olive oil works well with this dish.*

HERB POLENTA

SERVES 6
COOKING TIME: 35 MINUTES

- 10 OUNCES (300 G) POLENTA
- 2 OUNCES (50 G) BUTTER
- 2 OR 3 SPRIGS FRESH THYME LEAVES
- 1 SMALL BUNCH FRESH PARSLEY, CHOPPED
- 1 BUNCH FRESH BASIL LEAVES, CHOPPED, DIVIDED
- OLIVE OIL
- 6 TOMATOES, SLICED THICK
- SALT, TO TASTE

1. Boil about 4½ cups of water with a pinch of salt. Slowly add polenta, turn heat to low, and cook for about 25 to 30 minutes (or less if it's instant polenta), stirring constantly.

2. When polenta has a thick consistency, stir in butter, thyme, parsley, and half the basil. Mix well. When everything is blended, pour into a square casserole dish to cool.

3. When polenta has cooled, cut into 2- x 2-inch (5- x 5-cm) squares while still in the dish.

4. Lightly oil the plancha. Brown the polenta squares and tomatoes, about 2 minutes on each side. Place the polenta on a serving dish. Place a slice of tomato and 1 or 2 basil leaves on each piece and serve.

POTATOES AND ANCHOVIES

SERVES 6
COOKING TIME: 24 MINUTES

- **6** MEDIUM-SIZED POTATOES
- SALT, TO TASTE
- PEPPER, TO TASTE
- **1** (8.5-OUNCE [250-ML]) JAR SUN-DRIED TOMATOES
- **2** (2-OUNCE [43-G]) CANS ANCHOVIES IN OIL

1. Boil the potatoes in salt water for 20 minutes. Drain and let cool.

2. Peel potatoes and cut into medium-thick slices. Brown the potato slices on the plancha for 1 to 2 minutes on each side.

3. Line up browned potato slices on a plate. Sprinkle with salt and pepper.

4. Put 1 sun-dried tomato and 1 anchovy filet on each slice of potato. Hold together with a toothpick and serve as an appetizer.

73

EGGPLANT AND FETA PINWHEELS

SERVES 6
COOKING TIME: 5 MINUTES

- 3 EGGPLANTS, CUT INTO STRIPS LENGTHWISE
- SALT, TO TASTE
- PEPPER, TO TASTE
- 1 (8-OUNCE [200-G]) BLOCK FETA CHEESE, CUT INTO STRIPS ABOUT 1 INCH (2½ CM) LONG X ½ INCH (1 CM) WIDE
- 1 BUNCH FRESH BASIL LEAVES

1. Cook the eggplant strips on the plancha for 2 minutes on each side, then remove. Add salt and pepper.

2. Place a piece of feta and a basil leaf on each strip of eggplant.

3. Roll up each eggplant slice and pin with a toothpick.

4. Heat the pinwheels for 1 minute on the plancha.

SERVING SUGGESTION: *This dish works well as an appetizer.*

VARIATION: *Use goat or Roquefort cheese instead of feta—it's equally delicious.*

EGGPLANT AND GOAT CHEESE PINWHEELS

This recipe is done the same as above, just replacing the feta with goat cheese. Roquefort is an equally delicious substitute.

EGGPLANT AND SUN-DRIED TOMATO PINWHEELS

SERVES 6
COOKING TIME: 5 MINUTES

- 3 EGGPLANTS, CUT INTO STRIPS LENGTHWISE
- SALT, TO TASTE
- PEPPER, TO TASTE
- 1 (14-OUNCE [400-G]) JAR SUN-DRIED TOMATOES
- 2 OR 3 SPRIGS FRESH THYME LEAVES
- OLIVE OIL, TO TASTE

1. Cook the eggplant strips on the plancha for 2 minutes on each side, then remove. Sprinkle with salt and pepper.

2. Place 1 sun-dried tomato and a pinch of thyme leaves on each eggplant strip.

3. Drizzle with olive oil.

4. Roll up each eggplant slice and pin with a toothpick.

5. Heat pinwheels on the plancha for 1 minute.

SERVING SUGGESTION: *This dish works well as an appetizer.*

EGGPLANT AND ANCHOVY PINWHEELS

SERVES 6
COOKING TIME: 5 MINUTES

- 3 EGGPLANTS, CUT INTO STRIPS LENGTHWISE
- SALT, TO TASTE
- PEPPER, TO TASTE
- ABOUT 20 STRIPS OF SMOKED BACON
- 3 (2-OUNCE [43-G]) CANS ANCHOVIES IN OIL

1. Cook the eggplant strips on the plancha for 2 minutes on each side, then remove. Sprinkle with salt and pepper.

2. At the same time, cook the bacon for 2 minutes on each side.

3. Place 1 strip of bacon and 2 anchovy filets on each eggplant slice.

4. Roll up each eggplant slice and pin with a toothpick.

5. Heat the pinwheels on the plancha for 1 minute.

SERVING SUGGESTION: *This dish works well as an appetizer.*

EGGPLANT AND PRAWN PINWHEELS

SERVES 6
COOKING TIME: 5 MINUTES

- **3** EGGPLANTS, CUT INTO STRIPS LENGTHWISE
- **3** ZUCCHINIS, CUT INTO STRIPS LENGTHWISE
- SALT, TO TASTE
- PEPPER, TO TASTE
- ABOUT **20** LARGE UNCOOKED PRAWNS, PEELED

1. Cook the eggplant and zucchini strips on the plancha for 2 minutes on each side, then remove. Sprinkle with salt and pepper.

2. At the same time, heat the prawns on the plancha for 2 minutes (or until cooked through) on each side, then remove.

3. Place a strip of eggplant over each strip of zucchini.

4. Place a prawn on top, then roll everything together and pin with a toothpick.

5. Heat the pinwheels on the plancha for 1 minute.

SERVING SUGGESTION: *This dish is best as an appetizer with Tapenade (p. 45).*

SHRIMP-STUFFED MUSHROOMS

SERVES 6
COOKING TIME: 5 MINUTES

- 1½ POUNDS (600 G) UNCOOKED BABY SHRIMP, PEELED
- 3 CLOVES GARLIC, PEELED AND CHOPPED
- 1 BUNCH FRESH PARSLEY, CHOPPED
- SALT, TO TASTE
- PEPPER, TO TASTE
- OLIVE OIL, TO TASTE
- 12 LARGE WHITE MUSHROOMS, STEMS REMOVED

1. Mix the shrimp with garlic, parsley, salt, and pepper, and drizzle with oil.

2. Cook shrimp on the plancha for about 5 minutes turning frequently.

3. At the same time, place mushroom caps on the plancha. Halfway through (about 2½ minutes) turn the mushrooms over.

4. Place mushroom caps on a plate and fill with shrimp mixture.

SERVING SUGGESTION: *Prepare 2 mushroom caps per person and serve with Pink Onion Butter (p. 33) on the side.*

LEMON-STUFFED MUSHROOMS

SERVES 6
COOKING TIME: 10 MINUTES

- 2 POUNDS (800 G) WHITE MUSHROOM, STEMS REMOVED
- 3 TABLESPOONS (45 ML) OLIVE OIL
- JUICE OF 1 LEMON
- PEPPER, TO TASTE
- 1 CLOVE GARLIC, PEELED AND DICED
- KOSHER SALT, TO TASTE
- ½ LOAF FRENCH BREAD, SLICED AND TOASTED

1. Cook the mushroom caps for a couple minutes on each side.

2. At the same time, create an emulsion by vigorously mixing the olive oil with half of the lemon juice. Add pepper and garlic.

3. Line the mushroom caps top-down on a plate.

4. Pour the emulsion into each mushroom cap.

5. Sprinkle with salt and serve with bread.

BACON AND PEPPERS

SERVES 6
COOKING TIME: 15 MINUTES

- 2 RED BELL PEPPERS, SLICED
- 2 GREEN BELL PEPPERS, SLICED
- 3 ONIONS, THINLY SLICED
- ½ POUND (200 G) THICK-CUT BACON, DICED INTO SMALL PIECES
- SALT, TO TASTE
- PEPPER, TO TASTE
- OLIVE OIL

1. Mix the peppers, onions, and bacon in a medium bowl.

2. Sprinkle with salt, pepper, and olive oil. Mix well.

3. Pour whole mixture onto the plancha and cook 15 minutes, stirring frequently with a spatula.

SERVING SUGGESTION: *This dish can be served as an appetizer, a side dish, or tapas-style on crackers or grilled French bread.*

SMOKED SALMON AND ASPARAGUS

SERVES 6
COOKING TIME: 30 MINUTES

- 30 WHITE ASPARAGUS
- 6 SLICES SMOKED SALMON
- SALT, TO TASTE
- MAYONNAISE WITH HERBS (P. 29)

1. Cut off the tips of the asparagus and peel them, starting with the top point.

2. Boil asparagus in salt water for 25 minutes. Drain and cool.

3. Gently place asparagus on the plancha and brown them for 2 minutes on each side.

4. Put a slice of salmon on each plate then place 5 pieces of asparagus on top of each one.

5. Serve with Mayonnaise with Herbs.

81

VEGETABLE MISH-MASH

SERVES 6
COOKING TIME: 15 MINUTES

- **I** EGGPLANT, CHOPPED
- **I** ZUCCHINI, CHOPPED
- **I** RED BELL PEPPER, CHOPPED
- **I** GREEN BELL PEPPER, CHOPPED
- **I** YELLOW BELL PEPPER, CHOPPED
- **2** ONIONS, CHOPPED
- **2** TOMATOES, CHOPPED
- SALT, TO TASTE
- PEPPER, TO TASTE
- **2 OR 3** SPRIGS FRESH THYME LEAVES
- OLIVE OIL, TO TASTE

1. Place vegetables on the plancha and add salt, pepper, thyme, and oil.

2. Cook, stirring frequently with a spatula, until all the vegetables are tender.

3. Move to a dish and serve immediately with olive oil at the table for your guests to add as desired.

FRESH GARLIC

SERVES 6
COOKING TIME: 4 MINUTES

Fresh garlic, or Ajo Fresco, is a common appetizer in Northern Spain. It is quick and simple to make.

- 3 BUNCHES YOUNG GARLIC (YOU MAY SUBSTITUTE WITH GREEN ONIONS IF YOUNG GARLIC IS NOT AVAILABLE)
- OLIVE OIL
- KOSHER SALT, TO TASTE

1. Pull off the top leaves from the garlic.
2. Generously oil the plancha and cook garlic for 3 to 4 minutes, turning frequently.
3. Sprinkle with salt and serve immediately.

ONION RINGS

SERVES 6
COOKING TIME: 5 MINUTES

- 2 POUNDS (1 KG) ONIONS, PEELED AND SLICED INTO RINGS
- OLIVE OIL, TO TASTE
- KOSHER SALT, TO TASTE

1. Drizzle onion rings with olive oil.
2. Using a skimmer, place onions on the plancha. Cook 5 minutes, turning frequently.
3. Sprinkle with salt at the end of the cooking time and serve immediately.

SERVING SUGGESTION: *Onion rings go well with Anchovy Butter (p. 31).*

MINT TOMATOES »

SERVES 6
COOKING TIME: 10 MINUTES

- **6** TOMATOES, THICKLY SLICED
- **6** FRESH MINT LEAVES
- SALT, TO TASTE
- PEPPER, TO TASTE

Cook tomato slices 1 minute on each side. Sprinkle with mint leaves, salt, and pepper, and serve.

THYME TOMATOES

SERVES 6
COOKING TIME: 10 MINUTES

- **12** SMALL TOMATOES, CUT IN HALF
- **1** SMALL BUNCH FRESH THYME LEAVES
- SALT, TO TASTE
- PEPPER, TO TASTE

1. Place tomato halves on the plancha flesh-side down and cook for 3 minutes.

2. Carefully turn the tomatoes.

3. Sprinkle with thyme leaves, salt, and pepper.

4. Cook skin-side down another minute or two.

5. Carefully place tomatoes into a dish and serve with a fruit-infused olive oil on the side.

EGGPLANT À LA PLANCHA

SERVES 6
COOKING TIME: 10 MINUTES

- SALT, TO TASTE
- **6** EGGPLANTS, SLICED THICKLY
- PEPPER, TO TASTE
- SMALL HANDFUL FRESH PARSLEY LEAVES
- **2** CLOVES GARLIC, PEELED AND FINELY CHOPPED

1. Salt eggplants generously and let sit 1 hour.

2. Rinse eggplant and submerge in boiling water for 3 minutes. Dry eggplant well with a paper towel.

3. Place eggplant slices on the plancha and cook for 2 to 3 minutes on each side, carefully turning them with a spatula.

4. Move to a serving dish and sprinkle with additional salt, pepper, parsley, and garlic.

WHOLE SWEET GREEN CHILI PEPPERS

SERVES 6
COOKING TIME: 5 MINUTES

- 2 POUNDS (1 KG) SWEET GREEN CHILI PEPPERS
- KOSHER SALT, TO TASTE

Cook peppers on the plancha about 5 minutes, turning occasionally. Sprinkle with salt and serve hot.

SERVING SUGGESTION: *If the peppers are small, they can be served as finger food.*

PORCINI MUSHROOMS

SERVES 6
COOKING TIME: 4 MINUTES

- 2 POUNDS (1 KG) PORCINI MUSHROOMS, STEMS REMOVED
- PEANUT OIL, TO TASTE
- KOSHER SALT, TO TASTE

1. Clean mushrooms without wetting them by thoroughly rubbing them with a towel. Cut the caps into thick slices.

2. Lightly drizzle mushrooms with peanut oil.

3. Gently place the mushrooms on the plancha and cook for 2 minutes on each side.

SERVING SUGGESTION: *Season with salt and serve.*

FISH AND SEAFOOD

MUSSELS WITH PARSLEY

SERVES 6
COOKING TIME: 5 MINUTES

- 2 POUNDS (1 KG) LARGE MUSSELS IN SHELL
- 1 SMALL BUNCH FRESH PARSLEY, CHOPPED

1. Wash mussels thoroughly and place on the plancha, cooking for about 5 minutes.

2. Once the mussels have opened, sprinkle with parsley and remove from heat. Serve immediately.

NOTE: *This extremely simple recipe is a classic in tapas bars and* mariscos *(seafood) restaurants.*

CILANTRO CLAMS

SERVES 6
COOKING TIME: 5 MINUTES

- 2 POUNDS (1 KG) CLAMS
- 1 SMALL BUNCH FRESH CILANTRO, CHOPPED

1. Wash clams and open them up by heating on the plancha for about 5 minutes.

2. Sprinkle with cilantro and serve.

LOBSTER TAILS IN MADEIRA WINE SAUCE

SERVES 6
COOKING TIME: 13 MINUTES

- 6 LIVE LOBSTERS
- 2 OUNCES (50 G) BUTTER
- 1 SHOT (28 G) COGNAC
- 1 CUP (236 ML) MADEIRA
- 3 TABLESPOONS (45 ML) CREAM
- SALT, TO TASTE
- PEPPER, TO TASTE
- 2 EGG YOLKS, BEATEN

1. Boil live lobsters in water for 2 minutes. Remove from water and drain.

2. Separate the tails and cut in half lengthwise. Set aside.

3. Break open claws and chests; extract the meat and cut into small pieces.

4. Heat the butter in a frying pan and add the lobster pieces. Brown the lobster for 2 minutes.

5. Add cognac and Madeira.

6. Heat another 2 minutes, then pour in the cream.

7. Add salt and pepper, and simmer on low heat.

8. Meanwhile, heat the tails flesh-side down on the plancha for about 5 minutes.

9. Toward the end of the 5 minutes, add the egg yolks to the sauce. Heat sauce another minute without boiling.

10. Serve lobster tails coated with the Madeira sauce.

SPINY LOBSTER

SERVES 6
COOKING TIME: 20 MINUTES

- 2 OUNCES (60 G) BUTTER
- 2 CLOVES GARLIC, PEELED AND FINELY CHOPPED
- 1 ONION, FINELY CHOPPED
- SALT, TO TASTE
- CHILI POWDER
- JUICE OF 2 LIMES
- 6 LIVE SPINY LOBSTERS

1. In a medium pot, melt butter over low heat.

2. Add garlic and onion, salt, a pinch of chili powder, and lime juice. Remove from heat, but keep near the plancha.

3. Cut live spiny lobsters in half, and place each half flesh-side down on the plancha.

4. Heat for 2 minutes, then turn and place shell-side down. Cook another 15 minutes, brushing frequently with melted butter mixture. Serve immediately.

SERVING SUGGESTION: *For best results, serve each guest a lobster half, then cook the second half and serve everyone again.*

GARLIC PRAWNS

SERVES 6
COOKING TIME: 10 MINUTES

- ½ CUP (118 ML) OLIVE OIL
- 2 CLOVES GARLIC, PEELED AND CHOPPED
- 1 DRIED CHILI PEPPER, CUT INTO SMALL PIECES
- 36 PRAWNS
- SALT, TO TASTE
- PEPPER, TO TASTE

1. Pour oil into a medium bowl.

2. Add garlic and chili pepper to oil and steep for 2 hours.

3. Add prawns to marinade and refrigerate for another 2 hours.

4. Drain prawns and cook on the plancha, turning occasionally, for about 10 minutes. Serve hot.

PRAWN SKEWERS

SERVES 6
COOKING TIME: 10 MINUTES

- CURRY SAUCE (P. 34)
- 36 PRAWNS

1. Heat Curry Sauce.

2. Place 6 prawns on each skewer.

3. Put skewers on the plancha, making sure they lay flat, and cook for 5 minutes on each side.

4. Serve with Curry Sauce.

CRAWFISH

SERVES 6
COOKING TIME: 5 MINUTES

- 30 MEDIUM-SIZED CRAWFISH, HALVED LENGTHWISE
- SALT, TO TASTE
- PEPPER, TO TASTE
- LEMON BUTTER SAUCE (OPTIONAL, P. 34)

1. Place crawfish flesh-side down on the plancha and cook for 2 minutes.

2. Turn crawfish over and cook for 3 more minutes. Add salt and pepper to taste.

3. Serve crawfish plain or with Lemon Butter Sauce.

SCALLOPS

SERVES 6
COOKING TIME: 2 MINUTES

Espelette pepper is a mild type of chili pepper originally from the Espelette region in the south of France. It is a staple in Basque cooking.

- **18 SCALLOPS**
- **SEA SALT, TO TASTE**
- **1 SMALL BUNCH FRESH CILANTRO, CHOPPED**
- **GROUND ESPELETTE PEPPER, TO TASTE**

1. Cook scallops 1 minute on each side on the plancha.

2. Season scallops with sea salt, cilantro, and Espelette pepper, and serve.

SERVING SUGGESTION: *This dish is so delicious, there's truly no need to use additional ingredients. Serve with a simple arugula salad.*

CALAMARI WITH VEGETABLES

SERVES 6
COOKING TIME: 20 MINUTES

- 2 POUNDS (1 KG) CALAMARI, WASHED AND CUT INTO PIECES
- 2 ONIONS, MINCED
- 2 TOMATOES, SEEDED AND CUT INTO LARGE CUBES
- 1 GREEN BELL PEPPER, DICED
- 1 RED BELL PEPPER, DICED
- 2 CLOVES GARLIC, PEELED AND MINCED
- SALT, TO TASTE
- PEPPER, TO TASTE
- OLIVE OIL, TO TASTE

1. Place calamari and vegetables on the plancha. Season with garlic, salt, and pepper.

2. Cook while stirring frequently with a spatula for 15 to 20 minutes.

3. While cooking, drizzle some olive oil onto the plancha.

SERVING SUGGESTION: *Calamari and vegetables should be served nicely browned.*

BABY SQUID AND ANCHOVIES

SERVES 6
COOKING TIME: 10 MINUTES

- 2 POUNDS (1 KG) BABY SQUID, CLEANED
- 2 (2-OUNCE [43-G]) CANS ANCHOVIES IN OIL, CUT INTO SMALL PIECES
- OLIVE OIL, TO TASTE
- SALT, TO TASTE
- 1 TEASPOON (5 ML) GROUND ESPELETTE PEPPER

1. Place baby squid in a dish. Add anchovies and a drizzle of olive oil. Mix well and let marinate 15 minutes.

2. Pour mixture on the plancha and cook for about 10 minutes, stirring occasionally.

3. Season lightly with salt and Espelette pepper, and serve.

CUTTLEFISH WITH AIOLI

SERVES 6
COOKING TIME: 15 MINUTES

- **6** CUTTLEFISH, CLEANED WELL
- SALT, TO TASTE
- FRESH PARSLEY, CHOPPED, TO TASTE
- AIOLI SAUCE (P. 25)

1. In a large pot, bring water to a boil. Drop in cuttlefish and boil for 5 minutes. Drain and dry fish.

2. Cook cuttlefish whole on the plancha for 10 minutes, turning occasionally.

3. Sprinkle with salt and parsley.

4. Serve with Aioli Sauce.

CUTTLEFISH WITH TAPENADE

SERVES 6
COOKING TIME: 15 MINUTES

- 6 CUTTLEFISH, CLEANED WELL
- SALT, TO TASTE
- TAPENADE (P. 45)

1. In a large pot, bring water to a boil. Drop in cuttlefish and boil for 5 minutes. Drain and dry fish.

2. Cook cuttlefish whole on the plancha for 10 minutes, turning occasionally.

3. Sprinkle with salt.

4. Stuff each cuttlefish with a heaping tablespoon of Tapenade and serve.

SARDINE FILETS

SERVES 6
COOKING TIME: 6 MINUTES

- 18 LARGE SARDINES
- KOSHER SALT, TO TASTE

1. Cut off the sardine heads and cut the bodies in half lengthwise, making sure the halves aren't separated completely.

2. Gut fish and remove backbones.

3. Cook sardines for 2 to 3 minutes on each side.

4. Place on a serving plate and season with salt. Serve hot.

SARDINES IN VINEGAR

SERVES 6
COOKING TIME: 4 MINUTES

- 30 SARDINES
- SALT, TO TASTE
- BALSAMIC VINEGAR, TO TASTE

1. Gut the sardines, keeping the scales on the flesh. Rub them with a towel to dry and clean.

2. Cook sardines on the plancha for 3 to 4 minutes, turning midway through cooking. Lightly salt while cooking.

3. Drizzle with Balsamic vinegar before serving.

ANCHOVIES AND SALT

SERVES 6
COOKING TIME: 6 MINUTES

- 2 POUNDS (1 KG) ANCHOVIES
- KOSHER SALT TO COVER ANCHOVIES

1. Gut the anchovies, keeping the scales on the flesh.

2. In a bowl, lay down a layer of anchovies, then a layer of salt, followed by a layer of anchovies and another layer of salt. Let sit 30 minutes.

3. Remove anchovies from salt and towel them off one by one.

4. Cook on the plancha for 3 minutes per side.

FISH AND SEAFOOD

105

PLANCHA

ASIAN TUNA

SERVES 6
COOKING TIME: 12 MINUTES

- 3 TUNA STEAKS
- ASIAN MARINADE (P. 26)

1. Marinate tuna steaks in the Asian Marinade for 1 hour.

2. Drain the fish and cook on the plancha for 6 minutes on each side.

VARIATION: *This recipe works for many types of fish including hake and sea bream.*

SEARED TUNA WITH HERBS

SERVES 6
COOKING TIME: 4 MINUTES

- 1 TABLESPOON (15 ML) POWDERED GINGER
- 1 TABLESPOON (15 ML) CUMIN
- 1 TABLESPOON (15 ML) PAPRIKA
- 1 TEASPOON (5 ML) SALT
- 6 TUNA FILETS

1. Mix spices and salt in small bowl.

2. Roll tuna in spice mix until fully covered.

3. Cook tuna on the plancha for 2 minutes per side.

4. Put seared tuna filets on a serving dish and let cool. Serve with salad.

TUNA WITH PEPPERS AND ONIONS

SERVES 6
COOKING TIME: 12 MINUTES

- 2 OR 3 TUNA STEAKS, DEPENDING ON THICKNESS
- 1¼ POUNDS (500 G) SMALL SWEET PEPPERS
- 3 ONIONS, FINELY CHOPPED
- SALT, TO TASTE
- PEPPER, TO TASTE

1. Place tuna steaks, peppers, and onions on the plancha.

2. Cook tuna 6 minutes on each side. Turn peppers and onions occasionally with a spatula until golden.

3. Season with salt and pepper. Serve tuna covered in the peppers and onions.

107

COD AND CHORIZO

SERVES 6
COOKING TIME: 8 MINUTES

- **6** COD FILETS
- SALT, TO TASTE
- PEPPER, TO TASTE
- **12** SPANISH CHORIZO SLICES

1. Cook cod filets for 3 to 4 minutes on each side. Season with salt and pepper.

2. Two minutes before cod is cooked, place chorizo on the plancha and cook 1 minute on each side.

3. Place two slices of chorizo on each cod filet and serve.

DILL SALMON

SERVES 6
COOKING TIME: 8 MINUTES

- **3** LARGE OR **6** SMALL SALMON FILETS
- **1** TEASPOON (5 ML) FRESH DILL, CHOPPED
- SALT, TO TASTE
- PEPPER, TO TASTE
- LEMON BUTTER SAUCE (P. 34)

1. Cook salmon for 3 to 4 minutes on each side.

2. Sprinkle with dill, salt, and pepper.

3. Serve salmon covered with Lemon Butter Sauce.

MARINATED SALMON

SERVES 6
COOKING TIME: 8 MINUTES

- 4 SALMON FILETS
- CHINESE MARINADE (P. 21)

1. Marinate salmon in the Chinese Marinade for 1 hour.

2. Drain salmon, keeping marinade for later use.

3. Cook salmon on the plancha for 3 to 4 minutes on each side.

4. Just before the salmon is cooked, drizzle with more marinade. Serve immediately.

HERB SALMON (PHOTO ON PP. 88-89)

SERVES 6
COOKING TIME: 6 MINUTES

- 6 SALMON FILETS
- 1 HANDFUL FRESH PARSLEY, CHOPPED
- 1 HANDFUL FRESH TARRAGON, CHOPPED
- 1 HANDFUL FRESH THYME LEAVES
- 1 HANDFUL FRESH ROSEMARY LEAVES
- OLIVE OIL TO COVER
- SALT, TO TASTE
- PEPPER, TO TASTE

1. Place salmon in a bowl or dish and sprinkle with herbs.

2. Cover salmon with olive oil and marinate for 3 hours in refrigerator.

3. Drain salmon pieces and cook on the plancha for 2 to 3 minutes on each side.

4. Add salt and pepper. Serve with salad.

SALMON WITH LEMON AND BAY LEAVES

SERVES 6
COOKING TIME: 8 MINUTES

- 6 FRESH BAY LEAVES
- 6 SALMON FILETS
- 3 LEMONS, SLICED
- SALT, TO TASTE
- PEPPER, TO TASTE

1. Place a bay leaf on each salmon filet. Cover each filet in plastic wrap and refrigerate 2 hours.

2. Unwrap salmon and remove bay leaves. Cook salmon on the plancha for 3 to 4 minutes on each side. Rinse and preserve bay leaves.

3. Toward the end of cooking, grill the lemon slices on the plancha, a couple seconds on each side.

4. Add salt and pepper then cover the filets with the lemon slices. Decorate with bay leaves and serve.

COCONUT TUNA

SERVES 6
COOKING TIME: 4 MINUTES

- 3 LARGE TUNA FILETS
- COCONUT MARINADE (P. 28)
- 3 LIMES

1. Marinate tuna in Coconut Marinade for 3 hours.

2. Drain fish and cook on the plancha 2 minutes per side, until pink. Serve with limes.

« LEMON POMPANO MAHI MAHI

SERVES 6
COOKING TIME: 12 MINUTES

- 6 WHOLE POMPANO MAHI MAHI
- 3 LEMONS, SLICED
- SALT, TO TASTE
- PEPPER, TO TASTE

1. Wash and gut fish. Dry well.

2. Make small cuts on each side of the fish and slip in a slice of lemon, then add salt and pepper.

3. Cook fish on the plancha for 5 to 6 minutes on each side until skin is a little crunchy. Serve hot.

SEA BASS À LA PLANCHA

SERVES 6
COOKING TIME: 20 MINUTES

- 2 OR 3 WHOLE SEA BASS (ENOUGH TO SERVE 6)
- 3 CLOVES GARLIC, PEELED AND CUT INTO THIN STRIPS
- 2 TABLESPOONS (30 ML) OLIVE OIL
- 3 TABLESPOONS (45 ML) VINEGAR
- SALT, TO TASTE
- PEPPER, TO TASTE

1. Wash and gut the sea bass. Wipe clean.

2. Place sea bass on the plancha and cook for 8 to 10 minutes. Gently turn fish over and cook another 10 minutes.

3. While sea bass is cooking, heat garlic strips in olive oil for 1 minute, then add vinegar. Heat a couple more seconds and remove from heat.

4. When the fish is done, place on a serving dish and cut in half lengthwise.

5. Remove backbone and cover with vinegar. Add salt and pepper and serve.

TWO PEPPER COD

SERVES 6
COOKING TIME: 10 MINUTES

- 2 POUNDS (1 KG) COD FILETS
- 3 RED BELL PEPPERS, CUT INTO THICK STRIPS
- 3 GREEN BELL PEPPERS, CUT INTO THICK STRIPS
- 3 CLOVES GARLIC, PEELED AND SLICED
- PEPPER, TO TASTE
- 3 TABLESPOONS (45 ML) OLIVE OIL

1. The night before serving this dish, soak cod in water for 12 hours. The next day, drain and place in a bowl or dish.

2. Add peppers, garlic, pepper, and olive oil. Marinate for 2 hours.

3. Drain fish and peppers. Cook together on the plancha for 5 minutes on each side. Serve hot.

HAKE WITH GREEN SAUCE

SERVES 6
COOKING TIME: 8 MINUTES

- 6 HAKE FILETS
- 20 CLAMS
- GREEN SAUCE (P. 42)

1. Cook hake on the plancha for 3 to 4 minutes per side.

2. At the same time, heat clams on the plancha until they are open.

3. Heat Green Sauce and place everything together on a serving dish.

CITRUS RED MULLET

SERVES 6
COOKING TIME: 8 MINUTES

- 2 LEMONS
- 2 LIMES
- 2 ORANGES
- 12 WHOLE RED MULLETS
- 1 BUNCH FRESH DILL, CHOPPED
- SALT, TO TASTE
- PEPPER, TO TASTE

1. Slice all citrus fruit.

2. Clean and gut the red mullets.

3. Roll red mullets in dill until covered.

4. Cook on the plancha for 3 to 4 minutes on each side. Season with salt and pepper. Halfway through cooking, place citrus slices on the plancha and grill each side until golden brown.

5. Place citrus fruit on serving dish and cover with red mullets.

RED MULLETS WITH SERRANO

SERVES 6
COOKING TIME: 4 MINUTES

- **24** RED MULLET FILETS
- **1** BUNCH FRESH PARSLEY, CHOPPED
- SALT, TO TASTE
- PEPPER, TO TASTE
- **6** SLICES SERRANO HAM, SLICED INTO QUARTERS
- BALSAMIC VINEGAR, TO TASTE

1. Roll red mullet filets in parsley and season with salt and pepper.

2. Cook fish and ham slices on the plancha for 2 minutes per side.

3. Place ham on a dish.

4. Put one red mullet filet on top of each ham slice.

5. Drizzle fish with Balsamic vinegar and serve.

HAM AND TROUT

SERVES 6
COOKING TIME: 10 MINUTES

- **6** WHOLE TROUT
- SALT, TO TASTE
- PEPPER, TO TASTE
- **6** SLICES SERRANO HAM

1. Wash and gut trout. Season with salt and pepper

2. Wrap a slice of ham around each trout.

3. Cook trout on the plancha for 5 minutes on each side. Serve hot.

MONKFISH WITH CHERRY TOMATOES

SERVES 6
COOKING TIME: 10 MINUTES

- **6** SMALL MONKFISH TAILS, SKINNED AND RINSED
- **1** POUND (**400** G) CHERRY TOMATOES ON THE VINE
- SALT, TO TASTE
- GROUND ESPELETTE PEPPER, TO TASTE

1. Cook monkfish tails on the plancha for 4 to 5 minutes per side.

2. Three or 4 minutes before monkfish is done, place the cherry tomatoes, still on the vine, on the plancha.

3. Cook tomatoes without turning for the last 3 to 4 minutes. Remove tomatoes gently from the plancha and place on a serving dish, with the vine still attached.

4. Add monkfish to serving dish. Season with salt and Espelette pepper and serve.

FISH AND SEAFOOD

PLANCHA

MONKFISH MEDALLIONS »

SERVES 6
COOKING TIME: 6 MINUTES

- 6 MONKFISH MEDALLIONS
- 6 SLICES BACON
- SALT, TO TASTE
- PEPPER, TO TASTE

1. Wrap a slice of bacon around each monkfish medallion. Pin in place with a toothpick.

2. Cook medallions for 3 minutes on each side.

3. Sprinkle each side with salt and pepper and serve.

MONKFISH CURRY

SERVES 6
COOKING TIME: 8 MINUTES

- 1½ POUNDS (600 G) MONKFISH FILETS, CUT INTO SMALL PIECES
- CURRY SAUCE (P. 34)

1. Cook monkfish on the plancha for 3 to 4 minutes on each side.

2. Remove from heat and cover with Curry Sauce.

SERVING SUGGESTION: *This goes well with basmati rice.*

SEAFOOD *PARILLADA*

SERVES 6
COOKING TIME: 10 MINUTES

- **6** SARDINES
- **6** SMALL HAKE FILETS
- **6** SMALL MONKFISH FILETS
- **6** SMALL SALMON OR RED MULLETS FILETS
- **6** PRAWNS
- **12** LARGE MUSSELS
- AIOLI (P. 25)
- MAYONNAISE WITH HERBS (P. 29)
- ANCHOVY BUTTER (P. 31)

This recipe consists of a wide variety of plancha-cooked seafood. The above list is neither exclusive nor exhaustive—it depends on what's fresh at the grocery store. This is a special and hearty dish.

1. Place all seafood on the plancha and cook, always starting with those that take longest. In this case, all the ingredients take about the same amount of time, roughly 10 minutes.

2. When the fish is cooked and the shellfish has opened, put it all onto one large dish and serve with sides of Aioli, Mayonnaise with Herbs, and Anchovy Butter.

SWORDFISH WITH LIME

SERVES 6
COOKING TIME: 8 MINUTES

- 6 SWORDFISH FILETS
- LIME MARINADE (P. 23)
- 1 BUNCH FRESH PARSLEY, CHOPPED
- PINK ONION BUTTER (P. 33)

1. Marinate swordfish in Lime Marinade for 30 minutes.

2. Drain fish and cook on the plancha for 3 to 4 minutes on each side.

3. Once cooked, move to a plate and sprinkle with parsley.

4. Place a pat of Pink Onion Butter on each filet and serve.

MEAT

BEEF RIB STEAKS WITH KOSHER SALT

SERVES 6
COOKING TIME: 16 MINUTES

- 3 BEEF RIB STEAKS
- OLIVE OIL TO COVER STEAKS
- KOSHER SALT, TO TASTE
- FRESHLY GROUND PEPPER, TO TASTE

1. Remove steaks from refrigerator 2 hours before cooking.

2. Lightly oil steaks and cook on the plancha for 8 minutes per side.

3. Once cooked, place steaks on a dish and cover with aluminum foil. Let sit about 2 hours.

4. Cut steak into thick strips perpendicular to the bone. Season with Kosher salt and freshly ground pepper. Serve immediately.

SERVING SUGGESTION: *These steaks can be served with tomato and mushroom slices grilled on the plancha for 2 to 3 minutes.*

RIB EYES WITH CREAMY GARLIC SAUCE

SERVES 6
COOKING TIME: 4 MINUTES

- **6 RIB EYE STEAKS**
- **SALT, TO TASTE**
- **PEPPER, TO TASTE**
- **CREAMY GARLIC SAUCE (P. 31)**

1. Cook steak on the plancha for 2 minutes on each side.

2. Season with salt and pepper. Serve with Creamy Garlic Sauce on the side.

SERVING SUGGESTION: *Steamed potatoes go very well with the Creamy Garlic Sauce and are a perfect side to this dish.*

RIB EYES WITH SPICY MARINADE

SERVES 6
COOKING TIME: 4 MINUTES

- 6 RIB EYE STEAKS
- SPICY MARINADE (P. 20)
- 1 ONION, MINCED
- 2 SHALLOTS, MINCED
- 2 CLOVES GARLIC, PEELED AND MINCED
- OLIVE OIL
- SALT, TO TASTE

1. Soak steak in Spicy Marinade for 1 hour. Remove and wipe excess sauce.

2. In a medium bowl, combine onion, shallots, and garlic, and drizzle with olive oil.

3. Cook the steak on the plancha for 2 minutes on each side. At the same time, cook the onion, shallots, and garlic mixture on the plancha.

4. Serve steak covered in the mixture and sprinkled with salt.

FILET MIGNON WITH ROQUEFORT SAUCE

SERVES 6
COOKING TIME: 10 MINUTES

- ROQUEFORT SAUCE (P. 36)
- 6 ENDIVE LEAVES, CHOPPED LENGTHWISE
- 6 (2.5-OUNCE [30-G]) PIECES FILET MIGNON
- SALT, TO TASTE
- PEPPER, TO TASTE

1. Heat Roquefort Sauce and keep warm over low heat until ready to serve.

2. Cook endive and filet mignon together for about 5 minutes on each side.

3. Sprinkle with salt and pepper, then serve endive and filets covered in Roquefort Sauce.

HAMBURGERS

SERVES 6
COOKING TIME: 7 MINUTES

- 2 POUNDS (1 KG) GROUND BEEF
- 1 SMALL BUNCH FRESH PARSLEY, FINELY CHOPPED
- 1 ONION, FINELY CHOPPED
- SALT, TO TASTE
- PEPPER, TO TASTE
- 6 HAMBURGER BUNS
- 2 ONIONS, SLICED
- 3 TOMATOES, SLICED
- 6 LEAVES OF LETTUCE
- 3 LARGE PICKLES, SLICED

1. In a medium or large bowl, combine ground beef, parsley, and onion, and season with salt and pepper.

2. Make 6 hamburger patties.

3. Grill the hamburger bun halves on the plancha for 1 minute. Remove from heat and set aside.

4. Cook the hamburgers for 3 minutes on each side. Halfway through cooking, place onion and tomato slices on the plancha.

5. When everything has cooked, assemble the bugers on the buns with lettuce, pickle slices, tomato, and onion.

SERVING SUGGESTION: *Top with ketchup or BBQ Sauce (p. 30) and some mayonnaise.*

SALTIMBOCAS

SERVES 6
COOKING TIME: 10 MINUTES

- **6** VEAL SCALLOPS
- **6** STRIPS SMOKED HAM
- **12** FRESH SAGE LEAVES
- SALT, TO TASTE
- PEPPER, TO TASTE

This is an Italian recipe that works very well on the plancha.

1. Flatten veal scallops and ham strips with a meat tenderizer or rolling pin; cut veal and ham strips in half.

2. On top of each piece of veal, place a strip of ham and one sage leaf. Keep in place with a toothpick.

3. Cook flat on the plancha for 4 to 5 minutes on each side.

4. Season with salt and pepper then serve.

SERVING SUGGESTION: *This goes well with Spicy Tomato Sauce (p 36).*

GINGER VEAL CHOPS

SERVES 6
COOKING TIME: 6 MINUTES

- **6** VEAL CHOPS
- **2** CLOVES GARLIC, PEELED AND HALVED
- SALT, TO TASTE
- PEPPER, TO TASTE
- **1** SMALL PIECE FRESH GINGER, GRATED

1. Rub veal chops with garlic halves.

2. Cook veal on the plancha for 3 minutes per side.

3. Season with salt and pepper and sprinkle with grated ginger.

VEAL BREASTS AND ESPELETTE PEPPER

SERVES 6
COOKING TIME: 10 MINUTES

- **12** VEAL BREASTS
- **1** TEASPOON (5 ML) GROUND ESPELETTE PEPPER
- SALT, TO TASTE

1. Cook veal on the plancha for 5 minutes on each side.

2. While the veal is cooking, sprinkle with Espelette pepper.

3. Add salt and serve.

SERVING SUGGESTION: *Simple mashed potatoes are a perfect side dish.*

VEAL LIVER AND SHERRY VINEGAR

SERVES 6
COOKING TIME: 6 MINUTES

- 1 VEAL LIVER, CUT INTO 6 PIECES
- 1 BUNCH FRESH PARSLEY, CHOPPED
- 3 ONIONS, FINELY MINCED
- SALT, TO TASTE
- PEPPER, TO TASTE
- SHERRY VINEGAR, TO TASTE

1. Sprinkle veal liver with parsley and cook on the plancha for 5 to 6 minutes, turning once halfway through.

2. At the same time, sprinkle the onions with salt and pepper, and cook on the plancha for 5 to 6 minutes, turning frequently.

3. Cover veal with onions and drizzle liberally with sherry vinegar.

ITALIAN SAUSAGE

SERVES 6
COOKING TIME: 16 MINUTES

- 1½ POUNDS (600 G) HIGH-QUALITY PORK SAUSAGES
- BBQ SAUCE (P. 30)

1. Roll up the sausages like a flat snail and pin in place with large wooden skewers.

2. Pierce sausages with a fork in several locations, then gently place the sausage roll on the plancha.

3. After about 8 minutes, carefully flip the roll using the skewers, and cook another 8 minutes.

4. Serve with BBQ Sauce.

SAUSAGE AND MUSTARD

SERVES 6
COOKING TIME: 8 MINUTES

- 12 THIN CHIPOLATA SAUSAGES
- 1 TABLESPOON (15 ML) MUSTARD
- 18 THIN SLICES OF PORK BELLY OR BACON
- SALT, TO TASTE
- PEPPER, TO TASTE

1. Pierce chipolatas with a fork then cut each link into 3 sections.

2. Cut a slit down each piece lengthwise and open; fill pieces with mustard then close.

3. Cut each pork belly or bacon slice in half.

4. Place a chipolata section on a slice of pork belly then roll them up together; pin with a toothpick.

5. Cook on the plancha for 3 to 4 minutes on each side.

6. Add salt and pepper. Serve as an appetizer or main dish.

PORK WITH SOY SAUCE AND HONEY

SERVES 6
COOKING TIME: 8 MINUTES

- 2 CLOVES GARLIC, PEELED AND FINELY CHOPPED
- 6 TABLESPOONS (90 ML) SOY SAUCE
- 4 TEASPOONS (20 ML) HONEY, DIVIDED
- 6 PORK CHINES OR FILETS
- SALT, TO TASTE
- PEPPER, TO TASTE

1. Mix garlic, soy sauce, and 3 teaspoons (15 mL) honey in a small bowl. Marinate pork in sauce for 1 hour.

2. Drain pork and cook on the plancha for 3 to 4 minutes on each side, depending on thickness. While pork is cooking, drizzle with remaining honey.

3. Add salt and pepper, and serve.

SERVING SUGGESTION: *White rice is a perfect side to this dish.*

MARINATED PORK

SERVES 6
COOKING TIME: 20 MINUTES

- 2 POUNDS (1 KG) PORK TENDERLOIN
- EXOTIC MARINADE (P. 22)
- 2 ONIONS, THINLY SLICED

1. Cut pork into cubes.

2. Soak pork in Exotic Marinade for 2 hours before cooking.

3. Drain pork cubes and cook on the plancha for about 20 minutes, turning frequently and sprinkling with Exotic Marinade.

4. About 10 minutes into cooking, add the onions to the pork on the plancha.

5. This dish is ready when the pork and onions are both caramelized.

PORK CHOPS IN RUM (PHOTO ON PP. 124-125)

SERVES 6
COOKING TIME: 10 MINUTES

- 6 PORK CHOPS
- 1 CUP (236 ML) RUM
- 4 APPLES, PEELED AND CUT INTO QUARTERS
- 1 TEASPOON (5 ML) GRATED FRESH GINGER
- SALT, TO TASTE
- PEPPER, TO TASTE

1. Marinate the pork in rum for 5 hours.

2. Drain the pork and pat dry.

3. Cook pork and apples on the plancha for 10 minutes, turning pork over after the first 5 minutes.

4. When the apples are browned, sprinkle with grated ginger.

5. Season pork with salt and pepper and serve with apples.

PORK TENDERLOIN AND PEPPERS

SERVES 6
COOKING TIME: 10 MINUTES

- **12** THIN PIECES PORK TENDERLOIN
- **2** FRESH BAY LEAVES, CUT INTO SMALL PIECES
- **2** CLOVES GARLIC, PEELED AND CHOPPED
- **2** SPRIGS FRESH THYME LEAVES
- OLIVE OIL TO COVER
- **3** LARGE RED BELL PEPPERS, SLICED
- **3** CLOVES GARLIC, PEELED AND SLICED
- SALT, TO TASTE
- PEPPER, TO TASTE

1. Sprinkle pork with bay leaf pieces, chopped garlic, and thyme leaves. Cover with olive oil and let sit 2 hours.

2. Cook the peppers on the plancha for about 10 minutes, turning frequently. Halfway through cooking, add the pork and cook 3 minutes on each side.

3. At the same time as the pork is cooking, brown the sliced garlic.

4. Season pork with salt and pepper and serve with garlic and peppers.

BARDED PORK FILET MIGNON

SERVES 6
COOKING TIME: 10 MINUTES

- 2 SMALL PORK FILET MIGNONS
- HERBES DE PROVENCE, TO TASTE
- 12 SLICES BACON

1. Cut filets into 12 medium-thick medallions.

2. Roll medallions in Herbes de Provence then roll a slice of bacon around each medallion. Pin with a toothpick.

3. Cook on the plancha for 5 minutes on each side, turning frequently, until well done.

PORK FILET MIGNON WITH PINEAPPLES

SERVES 6
COOKING TIME: 6 MINUTES

- 2 SMALL PORK FILET MIGNONS
- SALT, TO TASTE
- PEPPER, TO TASTE
- 1 OR 2 PINEAPPLES, DEPENDING ON SIZE, SLICED (YOU WILL NEED 2 SLICES PER PERSON)
- 1 TEASPOON (5 ML) POWDERED GINGER

1. Cut the filets into 12 medium-thick medallions. Cook on the plancha for 3 minutes on each side.

2. Season pork with salt and pepper.

3. Once you have turned the medallions, add the pineapple slices to the plancha and cook for 2 minutes on each side.

4. Sprinkle pineapples with ginger and serve with the pork.

RIBS

SERVES 6
COOKING TIME: 20 MINUTES

- 2 POUNDS (1 KG) PORK SPARERIBS
- 1 TABLESPOON (15 ML) OIL
- 1 TEASPOON (5 ML) TOMATO CONCENTRATE
- 2 TABLESPOONS (30 ML) WORCESTERSHIRE SAUCE
- 2 TABLESPOONS (30 ML) SUGAR OR HONEY
- 1 TABLESPOON (15 ML) SOY SAUCE
- 1 PINCH CHILI POWDER
- 2 CLOVES GARLIC, PEELED AND CRUSHED
- SALT, TO TASTE
- PEPPER, TO TASTE

1. Separate ribs into smaller pieces with no more than 2 bones per piece.

2. Mix oil, tomato concentrate, Worcestershire sauce, sugar or honey, soy sauce, chili powder, garlic, salt, and pepper in a small bowl.

3. Rub oil mixture on ribs. Let sit 4 hours.

4. Cook ribs on the plancha for about 20 minutes, turning and basting with marinade frequently.

5. Serve well grilled.

RIBS IN ORANGE JUICE

SERVES 6
COOKING TIME: 20 MINUTES

- 2 POUNDS (1 KG) PORK SPARERIBS
- ZEST AND JUICE 3 ORANGES
- 2 TABLESPOONS (30 ML) SUGAR OR HONEY
- SALT, TO TASTE
- PEPPER, TO TASTE

1. Separate ribs into smaller pieces with no more than 2 bones per piece.

2. Mix orange juice, sugar or honey, salt, and pepper in small bowl.

3. Soak ribs in this mixture for 2 hours.

4. Cook ribs on the plancha for about 20 minutes, turning and basting with marinade frequently.

5. Before serving, sprinkle ribs with orange zest.

PINEAPPLE HAM

SERVES 6
COOKING TIME: 6 MINUTES

- 6 SLICES PINEAPPLE, FRESH OR CANNED
- 6 THICK SLICES COOKED HAM
- SALT, TO TASTE
- PEPPER, TO TASTE

1. Brown the pineapple slices for 1 minute on each side and remove.

2. Cut a slit in the width of each ham slice then slide a pineapple slice into the piece of ham. Close ham with a toothpick.

3. Grill the ham for 2 minutes on each side.

4. Sprinkle with salt and pepper and serve without any accompaniment.

« LAMB KIDNEYS

SERVES 6
COOKING TIME: 10 MINUTES

- 6 LAMB KIDNEYS
- RED WINE MARINADE (P. 25)
- 2 OUNCES (50 G) BUTTER
- SALT, TO TASTE
- PEPPER, TO TASTE

1. Split open each kidney without entirely separating into halves; pieces should be held together by a membrane.

2. Soak kidneys in Red Wine Marinade for 4 hours. Drain and dry.

3. Butter each kidney then season with salt and pepper.

4. Cook kidneys on the plancha for 5 minutes per side.

NOTE: *Cooking time can be reduced if serve the kidneys rare or medium rare.*

LAMB STEAKS AND THYME

SERVES 6
COOKING TIME: 4 MINUTES

- 6 LAMB STEAKS
- OLIVE OIL TO COVER LAMB STEAKS
- 3 SPRIGS FRESH THYME LEAVES
- SALT, TO TASTE
- PEPPER, TO TASTE

1. Lightly cover the steaks in oil. Sprinkle with thyme leaves.

2. Cook steaks for 2 minutes on each side.

3. Season with salt and pepper.

GARLIC LAMB CHOPS

SERVES 6
COOKING TIME: 8 MINUTES

- 18 SMALL LAMB CHOPS
- GARLIC AND OLIVE OIL MARINADE (P. 20)

1. Soak lamb chops in Garlic and Olive Oil Marinade for 3 hours.

2. Cook lamb on the plancha for 4 minutes per side. The chops must be cooked to the point that the layer of fat surrounding them is very crunchy.

LAMB MEATBALLS

SERVES 6
COOKING TIME: 12 MINUTES

- 1 POUND (500 G) GROUND LAMB
- ¼ POUND (100 G) GROUND LAMB FAT (KIDNEY FAT)
- SALT, TO TASTE
- 1 BUNCH FRESH CILANTRO, CHOPPED
- 1 TEASPOON (5 ML) *RAS EL HANOUT* SPICE MIX
- 1 TEASPOON (5 ML) CUMIN
- 1 TEASPOON (5 ML) SWEET CHILI POWDER
- 1 PINCH SPICY CHILI POWDER
- 1 ONION, DICED

1. Combine lamb, lamb fat, salt, cilantro, spices, and onion. Knead for a couple minutes, then let sit 30 minutes.

2. Wet hands and roll mixture into meatballs, making sure each one is no larger than an egg. Keep hands wet as you make the meatballs so meat remains sticky.

3. Flatten meatballs and cook for 5 to 6 minutes per side on the plancha, until well done.

POULTRY

LIME CHICKEN (PHOTO ON PP. 148-149)

SERVES 5
COOKING TIME: 25 MINUTES

- 1 WHOLE CHICKEN, CUT INTO PIECES
- 3 ONIONS, DICED
- 1 BUNCH FRESH CHIVES, CHOPPED
- JUICE OF 3 LIMES
- SALT, TO TASTE
- PEPPER, TO TASTE
- 2 LIMES, SLICED

1. Place chicken in a medium bowl with onions, chives, and lime juice. Season with salt and pepper, then mix well and let marinate for 2 hours.

2. Drain the chicken and cook on the plancha for 20 to 25 minutes, turning pieces frequently.

3. Toward the end of cooking, place lime slices on the plancha and brown for 1 minute on each side. Serve chicken and lime slices together.

COCONUT CHICKEN

SERVES 6
COOKING TIME: 25 MINUTES

- 1 WHOLE CHICKEN, CUT INTO PIECES
- COCONUT MARINADE (P. 28)
- SALT, TO TASTE
- PEPPER, TO TASTE

1. Marinate chicken in the Coconut Marinade for 2 hours.

2. Drain, saving marinade, and cook chicken on the plancha for 25 minutes, turning frequently.

3. While chicken is cooking, heat remaining Coconut Marinade over low heat. When the chicken is cooked, drizzle with marinade and serve.

PAPRIKA CHICKEN WINGS

SERVES 6
COOKING TIME: 15 MINUTES

- 18 CHICKEN WINGS
- OLIVE OIL TO COVER CHICKEN WINGS
- 1 TABLESPOON (15 ML) PAPRIKA
- 1 TABLESPOON (15 ML) DRIED OREGANO FLAKES
- SALT, TO TASTE
- PEPPER, TO TASTE

1. Lightly cover chicken wings with olive oil and sprinkle with paprika, oregano, salt, and pepper.

2. Cook wings on the plancha for 15 minutes, turning frequently.

3. Serve well grilled.

CHICKEN CHURRASCO

SERVES 6
COOKING TIME: 25 MINUTES

- 3 TABLESPOONS (45 ML) OLIVE OIL
- 3 TABLESPOONS (45 ML) VINEGAR
- 1 TEASPOON (5 ML) PAPRIKA
- 2 PINCHES CAYENNE PEPPER
- SALT, TO TASTE
- 1 WHOLE CHICKEN, CUT INTO PIECES
- 2 CLOVES GARLIC, PEELED AND HALVED

1. Combine oil, vinegar, paprika, cayenne pepper, and salt in a small bowl.

2. Rub the chicken pieces with garlic cloves and soak in the oil and vinegar mixture for 1 hour.

3. Cook on the plancha for 25 minutes, turning frequently.

4. Serve well grilled.

LEMON CHICKEN BREASTS

SERVES 6
COOKING TIME: 10 MINUTES

- **6** CHICKEN BREASTS
- **2** ONIONS, SLICED
- **1** CELERY STALK, CHOPPED
- JUICE OF **2** LEMONS
- **2** LEMONS, SLICED
- SALT, TO TASTE
- PEPPER, TO TASTE

1. Combine chicken, onions, celery, and lemon juice in a medium or large bowl or dish. Let sit 2 hours.

2. Remove celery and drain chicken and onions.

3. Cook chicken on the plancha for 4 to 5 minutes per side.

4. Halfway through cooking, add the onions and lemon slices to the plancha, flipping 1 or 2 times.

5. Season chicken with salt and pepper and serve with onions and lemons.

PARSLEY CHICKEN BREASTS

SERVES 6
COOKING TIME: 7 MINUTES

- **6** CHICKEN BREASTS
- OLIVE OIL TO COVER CHICKEN BREASTS
- **2** CLOVES GARLIC, PEELED AND CHOPPED
- **1** SMALL BUNCH FRESH PARSLEY, CHOPPED
- SALT, TO TASTE
- PEPPER, TO TASTE

1. Cut chicken breasts into strips and lightly cover with olive oil.

2. Mix garlic and parsley in a small bowl, then roll chicken in mixture.

3. Cook chicken on the plancha for 6 to 7 minutes, turning frequently.

4. Season with salt and pepper and serve hot.

HONEY CHICKEN WINGS

SERVES 6
COOKING TIME: 15 MINUTES

- **18** CHICKEN WINGS
- HONEY MARINADE (P. 28)

1. In a large bowl, soak chicken wings in Honey Marinade for 2 hours.

2. Cook wings on the plancha for 15 minutes, turning frequently.

3. Flatten wings so they completely touch the plancha as they cook.

4. Serve once skin is crispy.

CURRY CHICKEN BREASTS

SERVES 6
COOKING TIME: 10 MINUTES

- CURRY SAUCE (P. 34)
- **6** CHICKEN BREASTS
- **2** CLOVES GARLIC, PEELED AND HALVED
- SALT, TO TASTE
- PEPPER, TO TASTE

1. Heat Curry Sauce in medium pot and keep warm over low heat.

2. Flatten chicken breasts and make a small cut in each using a knife.

3. Rub chicken with garlic then cook on the plancha for 4 to 5 minutes per side.

4. Sprinkle with salt and pepper.

5. Serve covered with Curry Sauce.

SPATCHCOCKED CAPON

SERVES 6
COOKING TIME: 25 MINUTES

- **3** CAPONS
- OLIVE OIL TO COVER CAPONS
- SALT, TO TASTE
- **2** TEASPOONS (**10** ML) FRESH TARRAGON LEAVES, CHOPPED

1. To spatchcock the capon, make a cut down the length of the bird, from back to front, between the two breasts. Open and gently flatten.

2. Lightly oil capon and sprinkle with salt.

3. Cook capon for 25 minutes on the plancha, turning often.

4. A few minutes before they're done, sprinkle each side of the capon with tarragon.

155

« DUCK BREAST FILET

SERVES 6
COOKING TIME: 10 MINUTES

- 3 DUCK BREAST FILETS
- SALT, TO TASTE
- PEPPER, TO TASTE

1. Make a deep cut on the skin side of each filet. Open the filets in such a way that a layer of fat (skin) is on each side of the meat. Using a knife, score the fat side with crisscrossing cuts. The lean meat should be in the middle, bordered on each side by the fat.

2. Cook filets for 5 minutes on each side.

3. Once cooked, cut into medium-thick pieces. Season with salt and pepper and serve soon after.

DUCK IN PORT WINE

SERVES 6
COOKING TIME: 6 MINUTES

- 18 DUCK BREAST STRIPS
- 2 CUPS (473 ML) RED PORT WINE
- SALT, TO TASTE
- PEPPER, TO TASTE

1. Marinate duck in port wine for 1 hour.

2. Cook duck on the plancha for 3 minutes per side.

3. Season with salt and pepper. Serve hot.

DUCK WITH MANGO

SERVES 6
COOKING TIME: 10 MINUTES

- **3** DUCK BREAST FILETS
- **3** MANGOES, PEELED, PITTED, AND CUT INTO THICK SLICES
- SALT, TO TASTE
- PEPPER, TO TASTE

1. Score the fat side of the filets with crisscrossing cuts.

2. Cook filets on the plancha for 5 minutes per side.

3. Two minutes before the filets are done, brown the mango strips on the plancha for 1 minute per side.

4. When duck is cooked, cut into medium-thick pieces. Season with salt and pepper and serve with mango strips.

CITRUS DUCK

SERVES 6
COOKING TIME: 6 MINUTES

- **18** DUCK BREAST STRIPS
- **2** LIMES, SLICED
- **2** LEMONS, SLICED
- **1** ORANGE, SLICED AND THEN EACH SLICE CUT IN HALF
- SALT, TO TASTE
- PEPPER, TO TASTE

1. Cook duck strips and fruit together on the plancha for 3 minutes per side.

2. Season duck with salt and pepper.

3. Serve duck covered with fruit slices.

BASIL DUCK

SERVES 6
COOKING TIME: 6 MINUTES

- **18** DUCK BREAST STRIPS
- BASIL MARINADE (P. **26**)
- SALT, TO TASTE
- PEPPER, TO TASTE
- **1** BUNCH FRESH BASIL, CHOPPED

1. Soak duck in Basil Marinade for 2 hours.

2. Drain meat and cook on plancha for 3 minutes on each side.

3. Season with salt and pepper.

4. Place duck in a serving dish and sprinkle with basil.

SERVING SUGGESTION: *The duck should be served medium rare.*

FOIE GRAS

SERVES 6
COOKING TIME: 4 MINUTES

- 1¾ POUNDS (**800** G) DUCK FOIE GRAS, CUT INTO ½-INCH-THICK (**1**-CM-THICK) SLICES
- FLOUR TO COVER FOIE GRAS
- SEA SALT, TO TASTE
- CRUSHED PEPPER, TO TASTE

1. Lightly cover foie gras with flour. Carefully place on the plancha and cook for 2 minutes per side.

2. Move foie gras to a serving dish and season with sea salt and crushed pepper. Serve immediately.

DUCK HEARTS

SERVES 6
COOKING TIME: 8 MINUTES

- **30** DUCK HEARTS
- **3** SMALL DRIED CHILI PEPPERS, ROUGHLY CHOPPED
- SALT, TO TASTE
- GROUND ESPELETTE PEPPER, TO TASTE
- SWEET VINEGAR, TO TASTE

1. Open the hearts in the middle and remove any filaments. Sprinkle hearts with chili peppers.

2. Cook hearts on the plancha, turning frequently with a spatula, for 6 to 8 minutes depending on desired level of doneness; they can be served medium rare or well done.

3. Toward the end of cooking, add salt and Espelette pepper.

4. Just before serving, drizzle with sweet vinegar and mix well.

SERVING SUGGESTION: *This dish can also be served as an appetizer.*

CUMIN RABBIT »

SERVES 6
COOKING TIME: 20 MINUTES

- 2 WHOLE RABBITS
- 2 TEASPOONS (10 ML) CUMIN
- SALT, TO TASTE
- PEPPER, TO TASTE

1. Cut rabbit into pieces. Cook rabbit pieces on the plancha for about 20 minutes, turning frequently.

2. Halfway through cooking, evenly sprinkle rabbit pieces with cumin, salt, and pepper.

3. Serve immediately after cooking.

HERB RABBIT

SERVES 6
COOKING TIME: 30 MINUTES

- 3 YOUNG RABBITS
- 3 CLOVES GARLIC, PEELED AND HALVED
- OLIVE OIL TO COVER
- HERBES DE PROVENCE TO COVER
- SALT, TO TASTE
- PEPPER, TO TASTE
- 3 TABLESPOONS (45 ML) VINEGAR

1. Split open the rabbits lengthwise.

2. Rub rabbit meat with garlic inside and out. Cover in oil and sprinkle with Herbes de Provence. Add salt and pepper.

3. Cook on the plancha for about 15 minutes per side, flipping frequently.

4. Once meat is cooked, drizzle with vinegar and serve.

DESSERTS

LIQUORED BANANAS

SERVES 6
COOKING TIME: 20 MINUTES

- 6 BANANAS
- 1 CUP (236 ML) ALCOHOL OF YOUR CHOICE (COGNAC, RUM, OR ANY TYPE OF FRUIT LIQUEUR)
- POWDERED SUGAR, TO TASTE
- POWDERED CINNAMON, TO TASTE

1. Using a large syringe, inject alcohol into the bananas, through the skin, in several locations.

2. Place bananas in skin on the plancha and cook for about 20 minutes, turning occasionally.

3. Split bananas open lengthwise and sprinkle with powdered sugar and cinnamon.

FRUIT SKEWERS

SERVES 6
COOKING TIME: 4 MINUTES

- **1** ORANGE
- **1** GRAPEFRUIT
- **1** BANANA
- **1** MANGO
- **1** APPLE
- **1** PEAR
- **6** SLICES PINEAPPLE
- POWDERED SUGAR, TO TASTE
- WHIPPED CREAM

1. Peel the orange, grapefruit, banana, and mango.

2. Cut all fruit into same-sized cubes.

3. Spear the fruit onto 6 skewers. Sprinkle with powdered sugar.

4. Cook the skewers for 2 minutes on each side.

5. Serve fruit warm with whipped cream.

RUM PINEAPPLES (PHOTO ON PP. 164-165)

SERVES 6
COOKING TIME: 4 MINUTES

- I PINEAPPLE, SLICED WITH RIND ON
- I CUP (236 ML) RUM
- POWDERED SUGAR TO COVER PINEAPPLE SLICES

1. Marinate pineapple in rum for 30 minutes. Drain and cover with powdered sugar.

2. Cook pineapple on the plancha for 2 minutes on each side.

3. Let cool before serving, so that pineapple is warm but not hot.

LEMON BUTTER CAKES

SERVES 6
COOKING TIME: 4 MINUTES

- ½ POUND (200 G) CORN FLOUR
- 1 TEASPOON (5 ML) SALT
- ¾ CUP (150 ML) WATER
- 2 OUNCES (60 G) BUTTER
- 6 TABLESPOONS (90 ML) SUGAR
- JUICE OF 3 LEMONS

1. In a medium bowl, combine flour and salt. Slowly add the water while stirring.

2. Knead mixture thoroughly until a supple dough is achieved. Make a large ball, cover, and let sit 1 hour.

3. Form the dough into 6 equal balls. On a floured surface, flatten each ball with a rolling pin. This should make pancakes about 4 to 6 inches (10 to 12 cm) in diameter.

4. Cook cakes on the plancha for 2 minutes on one side, then flip them.

5. Place a pat of butter on each cake. Once butter has melted, sprinkle cakes with sugar.

6. Cook cakes on the plancha for 2 more minutes. Drizzle with lemon juice and serve.

TOSTADAS

SERVES 6
COOKING TIME: 3 MINUTES

- 2 OUNCES (60G) BUTTER
- 6 SLICES WHITE BREAD
- 2 TABLESPOONS (30 ML) HONEY
- 6 PRUNES, CHOPPED
- 2 TABLESPOONS (30 ML) CRUSHED WALNUTS
- 2 TABLESPOONS (30 ML) ALMOND SLIVERS

1. Butter slices of bread on both sides. Toast bread on the plancha for 1 minute, then flip.

2. Spread honey on each slice.

3. Cover slices with prunes, walnuts, and almonds.

4. Heat tostadas for 2 more minutes and serve.

APPLE BRIOCHE

SERVES 6
COOKING TIME: 6 MINUTES

- BUTTER TO COVER BRIOCHE SLICES
- 6 BRIOCHES, CUT INTO 3 OR 4 SLICES PER BRIOCHE
- 5 APPLES, PEELED AND SLICED
- 3 TABLESPOONS (45 ML) HONEY
- JUICE OF 1 LEMON

1. Butter both sides of the brioche slices.

2. Grill the apple and brioche slices on the plancha for 2 to 3 minutes per side.

3. At the same time, heat honey and lemon juice in a small pot over low heat.

4. Put brioche slices back together, alternating each slice with a slice of apple.

5. Place apple brioches on dessert plates and sprinkle with lemon honey. Serve hot.

GRILLED MANGO AND COCONUT

SERVES 6
COOKING TIME: 6 MINUTES

- 6 MANGOES, PEELED, PITTED, AND CUT INTO THICK STRIPS
- ¼ POUND (100 G) SHAVED COCONUT
- 1 PIECE OF FRESH GINGER, GRATED, TO TASTE
- COCONUT ICE CREAM, TO TASTE

1. Cook mango slices on the plancha for 2 to 3 minutes per side.

2. Sprinkle mango with shaved coconut and grated ginger.

3. Serve with coconut ice cream.

ORANGE CROISSANTS

SERVES 6
COOKING TIME: 6 MINUTES

- 3 ORANGES, PEELED AND SLICED
- 6 CROISSANTS
- 4 OUNCES (100 G) CRUSHED WALNUTS
- 1 CUP (236 ML) TRIPLE SEC

1. Cut each orange slice in half. Grill orange half-slices on the plancha for 2 minutes per side and remove.

2. Slice croissants in half lengthwise and grill, cut-sides down, for 2 minutes.

3. Place 2 half-slices of orange and 1 teaspoon (5 mL) crushed walnuts inside each croissant.

4. Lightly drizzle with triple sec, close croissants, and serve.

INDEX